OTHER BOOKS BY WOLF LARSEN

Unalaska, Alaska (an autobiographical novel)

Travel around the World? Why Not?
(an autobiographical novel)

Pricks, Cunts, & Motherfuckers, The
Novel About New York City

I Have a Nightmare (short stories)

Eulogy for the Human Race (poems)

Most of Wolf Larsen's books can be
purchased at Amazon.com

www.WolfLarsen.org

Capitalism Sucks!

Wolf Larsen

authorHOUSE®

AuthorHouse™
1663 Liberty Drive
Bloomington, IN 47403
www.authorhouse.com
Phone: 1-800-839-8640

First published by AuthorHouse 04/13/2011

ISBN: 978-1-4567-2638-6 (e)
ISBN: 978-1-4567-2639-3 (dj)
ISBN: 978-1-4567-2640-9 (sc)

Library of Congress Control Number: 2011900898

Printed in the United States of America

For my great-grandfather James O'Boyle:

immigrant, miner, I.W.W. organizer, & strike leader.

About This Book

Much of this book is a series of "interviews". In these "interviews" I answer questions I imagine readers may have about the evil system of capitalism and what we can do about it. There's simply too much war, too much unemployment, too much poverty, too much homelessness, too many people working their rear ends off for miserly wages, too much racism, too much sexism, too much homophobia – there's just too much human misery. I realize I am no deep theoretician, but perhaps the reader will be thankful for that, as the book is relatively easy to read. I am no labor leader, but I have worked at both blue-collar and white-collar jobs. I am simply just another face walking down the street, and as I walk down the street I see that the world is filled with unemployment, racism, sexism, homophobia, poverty, etc. What can we do about it all? That's why I've written this book.

Index

A WORKERS BILL OF RIGHTS

1) Double the minimum wage! Full medical and pension benefits for all who work! Everyone who wants to work should have the right to a job!

2) Defend unions! Defend picket lines! Picket lines mean DON'T CROSS! Defend the picket lines against scabs and other scum by any means necessary!

3) Bring all American troops home at once! No more money for the war budget – not one dime! Spend the money in the war budget on social programs instead to improve the lives of Americans! No more wars! No more invasions! Put the American President on trial as a war criminal! Treat veterans with respect! For fair treatment, full compensation and benefits, and quality medical care for all veterans injured in America's wars! For the unity of rank-and-file soldiers and workers against the war-mongering politicians, generals, and war-profiteers.

4) For an immediate halt to all evictions and foreclosures! Housing must be a right for all!

5) End the war on drugs! Legalize all drugs! Free everybody who is in prison on drug charges!

6) Support immigrant rights! For full democratic rights for

1

all immigrants! The only Americans who are not "illegal immigrants" are the Native Americans!

7) Full equality for women! Fight for equal pay for equal work! Fight for free abortion on demand! Quality free child care for all working women! Support the Second Amendment so that women can protect themselves from violence! No to feminism – feminism betrayed the struggle for women's liberation when they jumped in bed with the moral majority and became puritans.

8) Treat gays and lesbians with respect! For full equality for gays and lesbians! For full democratic rights for all gays and lesbians – including the right to marry! Gays should have the right to defend themselves with the Second Amendment against violent homophobic thugs!

9) No to segregation! Fight for racial equality! Blacks must have full access to equal education and opportunities as whites. SMASH this racist capitalist system – which was founded by slave owners and slave traders.

10) Break with black nationalism! The black nationalists murdered Malcolm X. Today's black nationalists sell the black people out to the Democratic Party – which is just as racist as the Republicans!

11) Smash the KKK and the neo-Nazis with mass mobilizations of workers, students, blacks, Jews, progressive whites, etc. whenever the KKK and the neo-Nazis try to march! Defend interracial couples from violent white supremacists and

black nationalists! Everyone must have the right to date whomever they choose!

12) Defend the Second Amendment! All Americans should have the right to defend themselves!

13) For a living stipend for all students, writers, musicians, and artists! Defend the right of artists and writers to fully express themselves in their work!

14) Free quality medical care for all Americans!

15) For free quality higher education! Eliminate tuition! Make all higher education free! Cancel all student debt immediately!

16) For billions of dollars for AIDS research until a cure is found!

17) Break with the Democrats! The Democratic Party is no different than the Republicans. The Democrats are warmongers just like the Republicans! The Democrats in Congress voted for the wars in Iraq and Afghanistan. The Democrats escalated the war in Vietnam, and dropped the atomic bomb in Hiroshima and Nagasaki. The Democrats are attacking our democratic rights just like the Republicans! The Democrats in Congress voted for the Patriot Act. The Democrats attack unions – just like the Republicans. The Democrats are not the friends of black people! The Democrats opposed the Emancipation Proclamation, the Democrats supported the Counterpro program in the 1960s that murdered black activists, and in 1985 Wilson Goode (a

black Democratic mayor) murdered a dozen black activists and their children in cold blood!

18) Build a third party – a workers party – a party that will fight for all workers whether they are white or black, male or female, gay or straight, native-born or immigrant.

19) Freedom of speech for all! No to censorship – whether it's by politicians, the police apparatus, religious extremists, conservatives, or P.C. feminists/liberals!

20) Strike down the Patriot Act! Full democratic rights for all!

21) Support the struggle of workers! For the unity of artists, writers, and students with the struggles of the working class! For the unity of white and black workers, male and female workers, gay and straight workers, native-born and immigrant workers – all workers must unite and fight together for better wages, better medical and pension benefits, and a better tomorrow!

Break with the Democrats and Republicans! Form a Workers Party!

An interview with Wolf Larsen

Question: Do you support the Republicans or the Democrats?

Answer: Neither! The Democrats and Republicans are pretty much the same! The Democrats talk a lot of pretty words about helping working-class people, blacks, Latinos, and women. But after they get elected the Democrats pretty much do the same as the Republicans. The Democrats voted for the Patriot Act just like the Republicans, so the Democrats are attacking our civil liberties just like the Republicans. The Democrats in Congress voted for two wars at the same time – Iraq and Afghanistan – so you can see the Democrats are warmongers just like the Republicans. The Democrats vote for hundreds of billions of dollars a year for the war machine just like the Republicans.

Q. But don't you think you we should support our troops?

A. The same politicians that talk about supporting our troops are the same politicians that cut medical spending for veterans. The politicians – both Democrat and Republican

– use rhetoric about supporting our troops in order to launch all their endless wars. The best way to support our young people is to give them a free college education or job training skills. Let's stop sending our young people into war! If the politicians want war then let's send all the politicians themselves into war, and let's bring all the troops home. I hear a lot of soldiers are sick of being in the armed forces – they've been called back to Iraq and Afghanistan so many times that they're sick and tired of war. They thought they were going to defend our country, but instead they find themselves getting shot at in order to further the interests of oil corporations in Iraq or the interests of a corrupt government in Afghanistan.

Q. So you're a pacifist then?

A. No. But these wars only serve the interests of the privileged few, and those privileged few are not the ones doing the fighting and the dying.

Q. I see, but since you say you're not a pacifist, which wars do you support?

A. The Civil War to smash the Confederacy and the War for American Independence are the only wars I support.

Q. Not the Second World War?

A. By the time the American troops landed on the shores of Normandy the Soviet Union was already kicking the ass of Nazi Germany. The American entry into the Second World War was more about stopping the Soviet Union from liberating all of Europe.

Q. So you seem to be arguing that the Democrats are warmongers as you call them. But many people view the Democrats as historically being the party of peace – how do you answer that?

A. The Democrats market themselves as the party of peace in order to get more votes and fool the people, but their actions after they get elected are no different than the Republicans. It was the Democrats that got us into both World Wars I and II, it was the Democrats that dropped the atomic bomb on Hiroshima and Nagasaki, it was the Democrats that escalated the war in Vietnam. The Democrat John F. Kennedy attempted to invade Cuba and brought the world to the brink of a nuclear holocaust during the Cuban missile crisis. The Democrats may talk peace, but they are warmongers just like the Republicans. The Democrats are war criminals just like the Republicans. The Democrats have blood on their hands just like the Republicans.

Q. But the Democrats have put up a black man as candidate for President. A woman – Hillary Clinton – almost became a presidential candidate for the Democrats as well. Isn't that significant?

A. No it's not. We've been through this before – we've had black mayors, black judges, black cops, etc. The black mayors and black judges and black cops have pretty much done the same as the white mayors and the white judges and the white cops. I don't think a black President will be any different than a white President. The rich people will keep on getting richer, and everybody else will continue getting poorer. And these wars are never going to stop as long as the Republicans and Democrats are in power. You mentioned that the Democrats put up a woman for President – or nearly put up a woman up for President – but England has already been through that. They had Margaret Thatcher, and she was as ruthless as any man! She attacked unions just like male politicians, launched wars just like male politicians in the Malvinas or Falkland Islands, and attacked the poor and social programs just like male politicians.

Q. But there's at least one difference between the Democrats and the Republicans – the Democrats are more for workers and for the poor – isn't that true?

A. No it's not. The Democrats are union busters just like the Republicans. Democrats will call in the police and even the National Guard to break your picket lines and escort scabs into your workplace just like the Republicans. Hillary Clinton, who was supported by many union bureaucrats in the last Democratic primaries, well she supports union busting legislation like the Taylor act, which makes it illegal for many workers like the transit workers in New York to go on strike. And as for the poor it was under the last Democratic administration in the White House – Bill Clinton – that welfare was replaced with slavefare. It was the last Democratic administration in the White House that ended welfare as we know it, and cut off many poor women and children from the welfare rolls.

Q. But the Democrats are more for women, aren't they?

A. No. The Democrats in the White House have come and

gone and we still don't have equal pay for equal work. And how about free quality child care for all working women? The Democrats haven't delivered that, they're not even talking about it! Why shouldn't working women have free quality child care, they pay taxes don't they? But instead all we get for our endless taxes is endless wars and more wars, and also our taxes pay to keep over 2 million Americans behind prison bars every night because of the war on drugs. And by the way it was the Democrats under Clinton – the last Democratic administration in the White House – that presided over the biggest buildup of prisons in American history!

Q. So if you don't support the Democrats and the Republicans who do you support? Do you support the Green Party?

A. No I don't support the Green Party. The Democrats and Republicans put corporations before working people. The Green Party puts animals before working people! (Laughs) The Green Party and its kind are more concerned about the rights of some dog than they are about the rights of a working person – these so-called left-wing liberals put dogs above the working person.

Q. Left-wing liberals put dogs above the working person? Don't you think that's a slight exaggeration – or a big exaggeration?

A. Maybe, a slight exaggeration. (Laughs) But you know, there's a certain type of liberal that gets on people's nerves. They're all holier than thou with their political correctness, and they're so sexually puritanical with their political correctness that they sound just like the conservative Republicans that they're always criticizing. And on top of that they're gentrifying our inner cities and driving up the price of rent!

Q. So if you don't like the Green Party who do you like? What kind of political party would you support?

A. We need a workers party! A party that will fight for all working class people – regardless of race, gender, sexual preference, religion, national origin, etc. We need a workers party – a political party that will fight for quality free medical care for everyone, quality affordable housing for everyone, equal pay for equal work, equality for black people, equal rights for homosexuals and immigrants, a decent free education for all, double the minimum wage...

Q. Double the minimum wage? Are you crazy? The Democrats just raised minimum wage 50%. If we raised minimum wage again wouldn't that hurt the economy?

A. It would certainly hurt the profits of the big corporations and the rich people, but it would be beneficial to poor workers – the people who need it most. Everyone who works deserves a decent salary! If people are working for miserly wages there's a name for that: wage slavery. And if paying working-class people a decent wage isn't good for the economy then we need a different kind of economy – we need the kind of economy that pays working people decent wages, where quality medical care is free for all, where everyone has the right to quality affordable housing, everybody has the right to a job, and where there's equal pay for equal work.

Q. But that all sounds like pie in the sky – how do you propose to have the kind of society where people make decent wages, everyone has free quality medical care, and everyone has quality affordable housing?

A. It would take a revolution – a workers revolution.

Q. But wouldn't that be violent? Wouldn't there be lots of bloodshed?

A. Well, if the rich people all just said you workers are right, we've been screwing you too long, and so we'll give up our power and our money, and we'll let you working people run the show – well in that case there wouldn't be any bloodshed.

Q. Well isn't that kind of naïve – to expect the rich people to just voluntarily give up their wealth and power?

A. It sure is! A workers government will have to defend itself against violent elements who don't want to give up their wealth and power to the working-class majority. All governments are instruments of class oppression. Either rich people oppress workers, or the workers oppress the rich people.

Q. But hasn't that manner of thinking gone out of style? I mean the Soviet Union collapsed didn't it?

A. The Soviet Union was governed by a bunch of Stalinist hacks – it's amazing that the Soviet Union survived as long as it did! And under a planned economy the working-class people in the Soviet Union were far better off than they are today in capitalist Russia.

Q. But things in Russia are improving – aren't they?

A. Lately things are improving because the price of oil is up up up! The Soviet Union exports a lot of oil and gas. But even with oil and gas exports bringing in lots of money most workers were far better off under the Soviet Union than they are in capitalist Russia. The standard of living of workers was higher, the people had free medical care, the people had affordable housing, they had pensions, they had the right to a job...

Q. But don't you think freedom is more important than material things?

A. Do the people in capitalist Russia have freedom today? God forbid that a Russian should criticize the new czar of capitalist Russia! The news media has little freedom. Political parties are being repressed...

Q. But isn't that the way it was in the old Russia – I mean the ex-Soviet Union?

A. Yes. So when Russia went capitalist the workers lost the right to a job, the right to affordable housing, the right to free medical care, and lots of other things too – but they never had freedom of speech under the old Stalinist system and they don't have freedom of speech under the new capitalist system either. What we need is a workers democracy – not a Stalinist bureaucracy like there was in the Soviet Union. And the fact that workers in capitalist Russia have little freedom today is proof that capitalism does not bring democracy. In fact, here in the USA we have less democracy every year. More and more our country feels like a bipartisan dictatorship of the rich.

Let's Build Big Strong Powerful Unions! Union Jobs and Union Wages for Everybody!

An Interview with Wolf Larsen

Question: Why do you want to kick out the trade union bureaucrats, as you call them, and replace them with a militant leadership?

Answer: Because the trade union bureaucrats are always selling out the workers. The trade union bureaucrats are too close to management. What we need is to kick the union bureaucrats out and replace them with trade union leaders that are more militant. We need militant trade union leaders that will fight for the rights of workers! We need militant trade union leaders that will fight for better wages, fight for free quality medical care for all workers, safer working conditions, free quality child care for all female workers, equal pay for equal work, etc.

Q. Why do you say that the trade union bureaucrats are always selling out the workers?

A. Because that's what they do! Often when there's a strike the trade union bureaucrats don't want to have real picket lines that mean nobody crosses. In addition, the union bureaucrats often don't care about the concerns of rank-and-file workers. A lot of these trade union bureaucrats seem to be more concerned with what's best for management. Many of these trade union bureaucrats are too close to management, they're too buddy buddy with management. There's labor on one side and there's the bosses on the other and you're either on one side or the other.

Q. You seem to be very passionate about workers rights. Does this passion come from your own experiences in the labor force?

A. When I was in my teens and early 20s I worked in restaurants, supermarkets, and offices. Then I worked on commercial fishing boats in Alaska for nearly 2 years. On some of those boats I worked over 100 hour weeks. Because there was no union we got screwed lots of times and in all kinds of ways. We were virtually slaves. You have to work on a commercial fishing boat in Alaska to see what I mean. Later, I stopped working on the commercial fishing boats. I started working on the docks. The first jobs I did on the docks was throwing 44 pound boxes of frozen fish for 12 hour shifts. Each man had to throw 3 tons of boxes per hour – that was the minimum! We stacked the boxes in rows up over our heads to the ceiling in the cargo holds of ships. We worked in freezer holds that were cold – up to 10° below zero Fahrenheit (-25 Celsius). Having just gotten off commercial fishing boats I thought this kind of work was easy at first. And we even got a break every two hours! I thought that was great! It was nice having the union. Because I actually got paid for my work. On the fishing boats we sometimes worked for free. Anyway I continued working as a longshoreman or dockworker for the next 10 years. I did stevedore work, which was throwing boxes, and I also did container work, which was lashing barges and ships.

Q. Were you represented by a union on the longshoreman's job?

A. Yes, I was represented by the International Longshore and Warehouse Union or I.L.W.U.

Q. That's supposed to be a good union!

A. It's one of the most powerful unions in the country. Maybe it's better than other unions, but as far as our own union local was concerned, well we used to call the union business agent Lameass. Lameass was his nickname. He was the main union bureaucrat in our port. Whenever we rank-and-file workers would say we want such and such changed the answer of Lameass was that that wouldn't be good for management. That union bureaucrat was more concerned about management than he was about us workers. What made things even crazier is that we were casuals. Even though we paid union dues we weren't actually members of the union. Anyway, I worked as a longshoreman in the port of Dutch Harbor Alaska on a seasonal basis for 10 years. I put in long hours twice a year – up to 100 hour weeks – and I took a lot of the year off to write and travel.

Q. What was being represented by the I.L.W.U. like?

A. In some ways it was good, real good. The pay was good.

If you got fired you only got fired for that day. You could come back the next day to work again. They couldn't get rid of you just because maybe some asshole foremen didn't like you. As long as you showed up on time and did your job it was difficult for them to fire you. That was good. They couldn't just replace you with their cousin, or their drinking buddy, or whatever. That was because there was a powerful union. The union controlled hiring. However, the people who lead our union local were very lame. I remember walking the picket line and watching scabs do our job. There was no effort to stop the scabs from doing our job. Instead of making a serious effort to unionize all of the dockworkers in the port the union would try to organize people in other lines of work that had nothing to do with the port because I guess that was easier. It was pathetic! The union gave away a lot of our work on a silver platter. Lots of work in that port that used to be union is now non-union.

Q. I see, and you feel that most trade union bureaucrats are pretty lame?

A. Most of the trade union bureaucrats are a bunch of Lameasses! What we need is a militant trade union leadership that is not afraid of leading a real strike. We need picket lines where nobody crosses! Scabbing should be hazardous to one's health! Massive picket lines should be set up everywhere where there is no union. Everything should be unionized!

Q. Everything should be unionized? Even small businesses?

A. Not necessarily small businesses. But what I mean is all major industry should be unionized. All major employers in the country should be unionized. All large employers should be unionized. Unions mean better wages for workers. Unions mean better benefits for the workers. Unions mean better job protection for the workers. In a strong union you can't be fired just because the manager doesn't like you. They have to have just cause to fire you if the union is strong.

Q. Many trade union officials make six-figure incomes. How do you feel about that?

A. I think that's awful! Trade union officials should only make as much as the workers that they represent! If the trade union officials make more than the workers then they don't have the lifestyle of the workers, they get out of touch with the workers, they don't understand the workers. Trade union officials should only make as much as the workers they represent. If the trade union officials decide they want to make more money than they better fight to raise the wages of the workers they represent as well.

Q. Many trade union officials have close ties to the Democratic Party. How do you feel about that?

A. I think it sucks! The Democratic Party doesn't care about workers anymore than the Republicans! The Democrats are a bunch of two-faced so-and-so's just like the Republicans are. We're basically living under a democracy of the rich. And both parties represent the interests of the rich. The Democrats call out the police against picket lines just like the Republicans. The Democrats support union busting legislation just like the Republicans. The Democrats aren't our friends. All that money that the trade union bureaucrats are giving to the Democratic Party is a complete waste of our hard-earned dollars. Instead of giving our money to the Democrats the unions should put the money in a strike fund, so the workers can go on strike whenever they have to!

Q . Some people say that unions are bad for the economy. How do you feel about that?

A. Unions are bad for the rich people's economy, but unions are good for the working people's economy. Unions put money into the pockets of working people.

Q. But isn't it true that unions impose a bunch of complicated rules on the workplace?

A. Many of those rules are there for a reason. For example there was a rule in our longshore union that if we worked after midnight the employer had to pay us extra money. That was an incentive to send everyone home at midnight. That way everyone could go home and make their spouses happy. Keeping their spouses happy helps keep marriages together. And the longshoremen can get some sleep. We're talking about a quality-of-life issue here. There were other realities too. Management was more concerned about production and less concerned about safety. Since it was the workers getting injured management didn't care about safety rules as much as we did. There were a lot of rules about safety, because safety was very important to us. Also, we didn't want management to practice favoritism in hiring. And that's why the union hall controlled hiring. Hiring was based on seniority.

Q. Why shouldn't management be able to hire whoever they want to?

A. In our port management didn't do the hiring. The union hall did the hiring. Jobs are given out based on seniority. Once all the people with seniority had jobs the new guys got a chance. Actually, giving out work on the basis of seniority made it more difficult for the employers to practice discrimination. Giving out work based on seniority gave more opportunities for blacks, women, gays, and anybody else management might discriminate against. Anybody who was capable could do the job. When the union hall controls hiring there's less discrimination. The workers feel more secure, because since advancement is based on seniority you don't need to worry as much about being in the good graces of the boss. There's no reason to kiss the ass of the boss. Kissing the ass of the boss won't help you. The only thing that will help you is doing your job and doing it right, and always showing up on time, etc.

Q. What other advantages did you find in a union job?

A. Union jobs are safer. By having a powerful union to back you up you felt more confident to refuse to do something that is not safe. (Our job was very dangerous.) In the beginning I worked many nonunion jobs in the port because I didn't have much seniority and those nonunion jobs were a lot more dangerous than the union jobs.

Q. What do you think should be done about corruption in the unions?

A. If there's some corruption in some unions it's up to the workers to clean house. The best way to clean house is for the workers to kick out the union bureaucrats that are corrupt.

Q. You don't think the government should intervene, to help make corrupt unions cleaner?

A. Absolutely not! Because the government doesn't care about making the unions cleaner. The government intervenes in unions to weaken them! The government is hostile to unions. The government makes these claims about corruption – which may or may not be valid – but the government makes these claims of corruption because the government wants to take over the unions and weaken them. Our own government is very corrupt. You're always reading about some corrupt politician. Who the hell are these corrupt politicians to be complaining about corruption in the unions?? The government should keep its hands off the unions! The unions belong to working people! The unions don't belong to the government! The working people must fight to keep the government out of our unions.

Q. If the government decides to take over a union or take over union local what can working people do about it?

A. They can protest. They can also go on strike. They can stage slowdowns. Workers in other industries and workplaces can stage sympathy strikes. There can even be general strikes – which would involve all the workers in an entire city or nation or industry.

Q. Why should workers in other industries and workplaces stage sympathy strikes?

A. Because if the government takes over a union then the government can later take over other unions too. An injury to one is an injury to all! It's in the self-interest of all workers to stand together and fight together. Workers are stronger that way! At any rate the strike, the general strike, the sitdown strike, slowdowns, protests, sympathy strikes – these are some of the tools with which the working class can defend itself and make demands. The working class can use these tools – such as the various types of strikes, including general strikes – to demand free quality medical care for all, better public schools for the workers' children, the release of political prisoners, etc. The working class can make powerful statements with these methods – and other methods too! For example, longshoreman and truck drivers and railroad workers can make a powerful statement by hot-cargoing all armaments destined for the wars.

Q. What is hot-cargoing?

A. It's when workers refuse to handle cargo – such as in the case of the war – workers refuse to ship and transport armaments. Hot-cargoing can also be used against companies that hire scabs. Railway workers, truck drivers, longshoremen, and warehousemen can refuse to handle cargo made by scabs.

Q. When many people think of unions they think of something outdated – don't you think that unions are now outdated?

A. How could unions be outdated when so many people are working so hard for such miserly wages? How could unions be outdated when so many workers on this planet don't even have medical insurance? And many times the medical insurance that the workers have doesn't even pay their medical bills – so obviously unions are not outdated when such basic concerns as decent wages and decent medical benefits are not even being met by the employers. The object of the employers is to pay workers as little as possible. Many workers don't even get a break at work – not even a 15 minute coffee break. If you take a 15 minute coffee break you get fired. The basic rights of workers are being trampled upon. That's why we need unions more than ever!

Q. But if the workers demand better wages and medical benefits won't the employers react by just moving more jobs overseas?

A. That's why you need unions! To fight to stop the employers from moving jobs overseas! If you lay down and play dead without a fight what will that get you – nothing! We shouldn't just give away jobs to the employers on a silver platter. We need unions in order to fight to *keep* our jobs. Ultimately, in order to assure jobs for everyone at decent wages we will need to have a workers revolution. Because under the capitalist system workers will always get screwed. But in the meantime we need unions to defend ourselves.

Q. Unions seem to be mostly confined to industrial jobs. Unions don't seem appropriate for non-industrial jobs – isn't that true?

A. You can organize lots of jobs with unions! The fact is 60% of Americans want unions in their workplace. However only 13% of the American workforce is unionized. That's because the bosses are engaging in all this union busting! It's also because the union bureaucrats are selling the workers out all the time. Also the government is on side of the bosses. For these reasons only 13% of the American workforce is unionized. But you can organize all kinds of workplaces. Supermarkets have been organized. Everything can be organized. Stores can be organized and made union. Chain restaurants like McDonald's can be unionized. Offices can be unionized. Office workers – many of them – are not well-paid. Many office workers get fired if they take a 15 minute coffee break. Many office workers don't receive benefits. Many office workers get fired for the slightest little petty thing! Many office buildings are just white-collar sweatshops. That's why we need unions in office jobs as well! You can unionize almost everything! Unions will bring better wages and more job security, because it will be more difficult for the employer to fire somebody without just cause.

Why Should Soldiers and Veterans Support A Workers Revolution?

An Interview with Wolf Larsen

Question: Why should soldiers support a workers revolution?

Answer: Many soldiers – especially American soldiers – are sick and tired of all these wars. Communists believe in peace. We are against war.

Q. Are you a communist?

A. I am a communist sympathizer. I'm not an actual communist because I'm not a member of any political group.

Q. Why should veterans support a workers revolution?

A. Not all veterans are being well treated by our government. Veterans who have fought for our nation and come back injured or disabled should receive help from the government. But instead of receiving help from the government there are many veterans who are receiving endless bureaucratic obstacles, instead of the help that they need. Communists believe that veterans should receive the help and benefits that they deserve! Veterans should receive quality free medical care for the rest of their lives. Veteran hospitals have to be improved! Veterans should also receive any benefits they need, especially if they are not able to work. Whatever help the veterans may need to cope with the stress from war memories and experiences than the government should help them with that too. Communists believe in fighting for the rights of veterans!

Q. Many American soldiers have been sent back into combat over and over again. How do you feel about that?

A. I feel that our government is abusing the soldiers by sending them into harm's way over and over again! If you fought in a war and survived you shouldn't be set back again to possibly die or get seriously injured. Our government is not treating the soldiers with the respect that they deserve.

Q. But isn't that the duty of the soldier – to go to war?

A. That depends on the circumstances. We are currently in two wars at the same time – Iraq and Afghanistan. Both of these countries are halfway across the world. These wars have nothing to do with the defense of our country! These wars are more about the rich people and the politicians wanting to dominate the world. Our government tells the soldiers a bunch of lies. The soldiers who are sick and tired of fighting should be allowed to leave the armed forces right away if they so choose. Soldiers leaving the armed forces should receive all the benefits that they were promised by the government plus free medical care for life and whatever job-training they may need to adjust to civilian life. Plus they should receive a living stipend until they're able to get settled and start working.

Q. But don't soldiers already receive benefits from the government? Don't soldiers receive free college education and job training?

A. I think a free college education and free job-training should be a right for all young people all over the world – including in our country. I don't think that young people should have to risk their lives abroad in order to receive free college education and free job-training. The best way to support our young people is to make sure that they have the tools they need – like a college education or job training – so that they can lead productive and prosperous lives.

Q. After the Vietnam War some people spit in the face of returning soldiers and called them baby killers. How do you feel about that?

A. If some people engaged in that kind of ignorant behavior than that's disgusting. Returning soldiers should be treated with respect. I think actually it's *the government* that treats returning soldiers with disrespect! Many soldiers need help with medical problems that they have incurred during the war, but often instead of receiving help for their medical problems they receive a bunch of bureaucratic obstacles. Some of these returning soldiers have health problems so serious that they are unable to work. Instead of helping them our government only gives many of them endless bureaucratic obstacles, and the soldiers wind up homeless as a result. Yes, there are homeless veterans living on our streets! They don't have a place to live. Obviously, our government is not helping some returning soldiers enough. The politicians and the four-star generals talk a bunch of pretty words about soldiers and veterans but when it comes to helping the soldiers and veterans that need help the government obviously falls short. Not a single veteran should be homeless!

Q. You say that soldiers and veterans should support a workers revolution. What connection is there between workers and soldiers?

A. Many workers are dissatisfied with the economic and political system because they don't have enough money to pay their bills, medical care is too expensive, the public schools for their children are often lousy, the rent is too high – the list of workers complaints just goes on and on. Many soldiers are not happy with our political and economic situation either. Many soldiers are sick and tired of being sent back into war again and again – they are being sent back to wars that have nothing to do with protecting America – wars that are more about helping the interests of the rich and privileged few. Many veterans returning injured from the war have trouble just getting the kind of benefits and medical care that they need and deserve. Both soldiers and workers deserve more respect. Both soldiers and workers have their complaints against the system. Both soldiers and workers would benefit from a society where there are less wars and more jobs with good wages and good benefits. And remember, soldiers are often from working-class families. The soldiers have more in common with the workers, and have less in common with the war-mongering politicians and war-profiteering rich people.

Q. I don't understand how soldiers would benefit from a society of peace. Isn't that what soldiers do – fight wars?

A. The soldiers are being made to fight wars that benefit privileged economic interests. The politicians are sending the soldiers into wars because the politicians have this crazy idea of dominating the world. Apparently these politicians in Washington think that they're in ancient Rome and that America is some Roman Empire. If these politicians want to dominate the world let the politicians and their children fight the wars! I think many young people join the armed forces for practical reasons – like getting financial help with a college education or simply escaping from a place where there are few opportunities. What we need to do is provide young people with real opportunities. Everyone – including young adults – should have the right to a job. Minimum wage should be doubled so that people can live a decent life. College education should be free. Under these circumstances with free college education, and everyone having the right to a job, with a minimum wage you can live on and still have some left over afterwards to have fun, then under these circumstances many young people would have more options in life.

Q. Are you a pacifist?

A. Absolutely not. Sometimes war is necessary, particularly in self-defense. I think the Red Army of the Soviet Union did a great job of kicking the ass of Nazi Germany!

Q. But you're against most wars?

A. Yes I am. Most wars are fought for the benefit of a privileged few. There are always politicians and dictators who have no problem sending young people to die just so that those politicians and dictators can advance their own power hungry interests. Too many young people's lives have been lost pointlessly in endless wars that only benefit a privileged few. As we all know war causes hardship and suffering and death and destruction. Why should the sons and daughters of working people kill each other just because they're from different nations? The soldiers killing each other on the battlefield often have more in common with each other than they do with the politicians, dictators, and generals who sent them into harm's way. Soldiers fighting each other should make peace with each other. The real enemy of the rank-and-file American soldier is in Washington, DC and on Park Avenue in New York. Park Avenue in New York is where some of the richest people in our country live. The rich are the people that benefit from all these wars.

Q. Soldiers who are fighting each other making peace with each other? Don't you think that sounds naïve?

A. No, not entirely. During World War I soldiers on the Western Front stopped fighting each other and made peace with each other. It all began Christmas Eve and continued on for a while. The soldiers refused to fight. Instead, the soldiers of the rival armies played soccer with each other in the no man's land between the trenches. Soldiers of the rival armies drank together. The vast majority of the lower-ranking rank officers did not have a problem with this. But when the generals stationed further away from the front heard that the two sides had spontaneously laid down their arms then the generals became furious and ordered the lower-ranking officers to make the soldiers shoot at each other again. Most of the soldiers on both sides were very reluctant to start hostilities again. I encourage soldiers and veterans and everybody else to learn more about this wonderful spontaneous peace between the rank-and-file soldiers on both sides of the Western Front during World War I.

Q. Weren't soldiers an important part of the workers revolution in Russia in 1917?

A. Yes they were. The Russian soldiers were sick and tired of the First World War. Originally, Russian soldiers had been very supportive of the war. But as the war dragged on the soldiers lost enthusiasm for the war and turned against it. The soldiers wanted peace, or most of them wanted peace anyway. The Russian workers were unhappy too. The workers in the factories were tired of working so hard for such low wages. They wanted better wages. They were having a hard time making ends meet. In the countryside there were many peasants living in poverty. In March of 1917 the Czar was kicked out and a reformist government took power. However, despite all the promises of this reformist government nothing changed. The war raged on, wages in the factories remained low, and the peasants continued suffering. So the workers, soldiers, and the peasants united together and they kicked out the reformist government and put the communists in power. The communists ended the war. Russia – or rather the new Soviet Union – withdrew from the war. The soldiers were able to return home.

The Race Question

An Interview with Wolf Larsen

Question: So what do you think of race in America?

Answer: Well, it doesn't matter what color a man is because white, black, or brown all men are ugly. It doesn't matter what color a woman is after you turn off the light. And it doesn't matter what color the President is because all these politicians stink the same. (Laughs) However, more seriously, race in America is bizarre. I don't even know where to begin!

Q. What do you think of black politicians?

A. They do all the same rotten things that the white politicians do. The main differences is that black politicians foster illusions in the capitalist system. But basically these black politicians carry out the bidding of the rich and powerful just like the white politicians.

Q. What do you think of the black experience?

A. Well, anyone who has read their history knows that it's been brutal. Black people in the United States have experienced four centuries of brutal racist oppression!

Anyone with eyes can see that black people continue to suffer oppression under this racist system – or at least most black people continue to be oppressed under this racist system. The fact that black people continue to be oppressed today can be traced back to the fact that the Democratic Party ended Reconstruction. Had the Democrats not ended Reconstruction black people might have achieved economic and political equality with white people in the 19th century! So you can blame the Democrats for the fact that black people continue to be oppressed today.

Q. But isn't it true that many whites are oppressed as well?

A. That's very true. At this very moment many white people are losing their jobs and being evicted out into the street with all these foreclosures. Many white people are working for minimum wage. Many whites cannot afford their copayments and therefore have to do without medical care. Things are very difficult for many white people in the United States of America, whether people realize it or not. However, things are even more difficult for the majority of blacks. Under capitalism the working class and poor whites suffer – the working class and poor blacks suffer even more.

Q. You point out that black people have had a very difficult history in the United States. But isn't it true that many working-class whites have also had a difficult history in the United States?

A. Undoubtably both working class whites and blacks have

had a very difficult experience in the capitalist United States of America. The cotton that was picked by black sharecroppers in the South was put on trains and brought up to New England where some of my ancestors worked in the textile mills. My great-grand-uncle began working in the textile mills when he was nine years old. My great-grand-uncle at the age of nine was working in the textile mills 12 hours a day six days a week. Another case in point is the Irish. When the slave trade was banned the ships that had been used for slavery were sent to Ireland where they picked up the Irish immigrants. One out of every seven of those immigrants died in the passage. The Anglo-Saxon landowners back in Ireland exported food from Ireland while the Irish Catholic people were starving. When the Irish Catholics came here to America they were viciously discriminated against by many of the Anglo-Saxons here. It's ironic that many people blame the Jews for everything, when in fact our country is being run mostly by a bunch of Anglo-Saxons. However, for every pillage and plunder rich Anglo-Saxon on Wall Street there's many many more Anglo-Saxons making minimum wage. So you have to keep it all in perspective. All working-class people of all colors and backgrounds are victims of the capitalist system. But however horrible the experience of working-class white Americans has been in the United States the black experience has been much worse. Our ancestors may have come here because they were starving to death. However, we must remember that the Africans who were forced to come here were not starving to death back in the old world – they were brought here in chains. And for centuries they were not even paid for their work! It is important to understand that black people – or most black people – in this country have suffered and continue to suffer a double oppression. As workers they suffer oppression, all of the same oppression that white workers suffer. But in addition to all that blacks suffer the oppression of the racist American color cast system. That system may not be written into laws anymore, but it still exists in many ways. It's important that white workers understand this and always stand united with the black worker against all aspects of racial oppression. It's also very important that black workers understand that white workers have many of the same concerns that black workers have – concerns like unemployment, quality affordable housing, quality public schools for their children, etc. Black workers must understand that the people who benefited from the slave trade and slavery were a privileged elite of whites. For example, the first time many northern whites ever saw black people was when they walked onto the plantations of the South in Union Civil War uniforms and said, "You're free". In the South the slave system was beneficial only to a small minority of white people who enriched themselves at the expense of black free labor. Most whites in the South were actually hurt by slavery. How can you demand better wages from your employer when you might be replaced with a slave who works for free? The slave owners manipulated the rest of the Southern whites against the black people in order to continue slavery and later sharecropping. The fact is most whites in the South had nothing to gain and everything to lose if slavery had continued. For this reason the Union victory in the Civil War was not only beneficial to blacks, but it was also beneficial to most southern whites, whether they realized it or not. After all, how are you supposed to compete with free slave labor?!

Q. So how do we end the racial oppression of black people?

A. First, black people have to realize that the capitalist system has nothing to offer them except more misery and racism. This government was founded by slaveholders and slave traders. This government will always keep most black people down. And if some black faces crawl up to high places (like they become politicians and judges and CEOs of big corporations) those black faces in high places will become collaborators in the racist system. Those black faces in high places will help keep most black people down, just like the white faces in high places. The only solution is to throw the whole racist capitalist system in the garbage can! The only solution is to smash the racist bourgeois government, and replace it with a workers government. A workers government will institute socialism. Under socialism everyone will have the right to a job. The minimum wage will be doubled. Everyone will have the right to free quality child care, affordable decent housing, free medical care, etc. This will be beneficial to white workers and black workers. This will be beneficial to white poor people and black poor people. Under socialism no one will be poor unless they're too lazy to work. There will be no billionaires or multimillionaires. This will be great for most black people. Everyone will have the right to a free quality education. Education spending per student will be equal in all schools across the nation. That is, black students will receive the same quality education as white students. Everyone, white or black will have the same chance in life. Under socialism, if you are smart and hard-working you will be able to achieve great things. Nobody will face the kind of obstacles that both poor whites and blacks face today. College education will be free for all.

Q. What do you think of affirmative action?

A. I favor affirmative action under certain circumstances, but not all. I think there will probably be a certain amount of affirmative action under socialism until blacks have economic parity with whites, and women have economic parity with men. However, hard work, personal abilities, and seniority will be very important factors in determining who receives promotions under socialism. When promotions are based on seniority and skills more black people rise to high positions. However, when promotion is decided by some capitalist boss or manager it seems that black people remain behind. This is what I have noticed from my own employment experience. When there is a strong powerful union there are more black faces in high positions. Having a strong powerful union makes it more difficult for some boss to discriminate against blacks. Basing promotions on seniority is good for women workers too, because it helps eliminate gender discrimination. Basing promotions on seniority makes many white male workers happy as well, because they don't have to worry about some back-stabbing ass-kisser being promoted to a better job before them.

Q. So it seems like you're in favor of some mixture of seniority and affirmative action – am I correct?

A. Yes. But let's remember that President Richard Nixon was at least at one point in favor of affirmative action. Richard Nixon liked affirmative action not because he liked black people, but because he wanted to undermine unions and because in union jobs there was often a strong emphasis on seniority as a means of promotion. Richard Nixon was no dummy, and in supporting affirmative action part of his game was to drive a wedge between minorities and organized labor. And as I just pointed out basing promotion on seniority is an excellent way to make sure that the playing field is equal for blacks. Seniority as a means of advancement is an excellent way to make sure there's no discrimination against blacks in giving out work and promotions. However, if two persons have roughly equal amounts of seniority then I favor affirmative action. But if someone has been on the job for two years and somebody else has been on the job for two months obviously the promotion should go to the person who's been on the job longer, as long as they are competent and have a good work ethic. Seniority is good. Where seniority is a strong factor in advancement black people are more likely to get their fair share of the good jobs. As far as affirmative action in education is concerned affirmative action should not be an issue, because all colleges should have open admissions. That means anybody white or black who finishes high school should be allowed to go to college. If someone needs to take remedial classes than they need to take remedial classes. But everyone should be allowed to go to any college they choose, except for perhaps a medical college where there may be special criteria besides just finishing high school or getting a GED.

Q. But wouldn't the quality of education go down if there were open admissions?

A. No. My alma mater is CCNY or City College of New York. CCNY has open admissions. CCNY has had more Noble Prize winners among its alumni than all of the Ivy League colleges on the East Coast combined.

Q. What do you think of black nationalism?

A. I would have to say that today's black nationalists fill me with disgust. At times they seem to act like Nazi storm troopers outside of Korean grocery stores. I have seen black nationalists act like fascistic thugs when they encounter interracial couples. I have been witness to the bullying thuggish behavior of groups of young men influenced by black nationalism and white supremacy. It seems like these black nationalists and white supremacist thugs need to be in groups in order to beat up one man. They are truly pathetic. However, I do not equate black nationalism with fascism. However, it is disgusting the way that thugs influenced by black nationalism act out in a manner similar to white supremacist fascists. But again I'm not saying that the black nationalists are fascists. However, both whites and blacks must have the right to defend themselves against these black nationalist and white supremacist thugs. I realize that not all black nationalists are thugs, perhaps most of them are not. But much of their race hate speech seems to influence the behavior of thugs. It seems like not since the Black Panthers and Malcolm X has there been a decent black nationalist. The Black Panthers were courageous defenders of the Second Amendment and the right of blacks to defend themselves against the racist violence of the bourgeois government. Malcolm X often told the truth about some things – like the nature of politicians. Malcolm X had nothing good to say about any politician white or black. And Malcolm X said, "When you vote Democrat you vote Dixiecrat!" I guess they don't make black nationalists like they used to. Anyway, within black nationalism there are inherent problems. Black people are now the *third* largest group in this country – after Latinos. If black workers do not unite with white and Latino workers then the black workers will be weaker. Either the white and black and Latino workers unite together, or divided the white and black and Latino workers will continue to be oppressed by the bourgeoisie. If black workers are sick and tired of a racist capitalist system of unemployment, low wages, inferior housing, inferior education than they are simply going to have to throw capitalism in the garbage can. In order to do that they have to unite with all workers of all colors. Black nationalism – like white supremacy – is against white, black, and Latino workers being united. When black, white, and Latino workers unite and do things together we can accomplish a lot. Maybe one day workers of all races united together will throw capitalism in the garbage can and replace it with socialism.

So What If the Next President Of The United States Is Black?

An Interview with Wolf Larsen

Question: A black man is the Democratic nominee for President. What will change if anything if a black man becomes President of the most powerful nation on earth?

Answer: Nothing. Absolutely nothing.

Q. Why do you say that?

A. Black politicians are pretty much the same as white politicians – that is black politicians keep black people and everybody else down just like white politicians.

Q. But don't you think this will be an uplifting experience for black people? To have a black President – isn't that something?

A. No it's not. There are many black people that accomplish great things – but black politicians are not one of them. Black musicians, black artists, black leaders like Frederick Douglass, black inventors like that guy that invented the traffic light – where would we be without the traffic light? These are black people that have accomplished great things.

On the other hand black politicians, like white politicians, accomplish nothing! The word politician might as well be a four letter word. (Laughs)

Q. But what about the pride that many black people will feel if there is a black President?

A. And maybe that pride will turn into disgust and disillusionment once the majority of black people realize that having a black President changes nothing. If the black majority continue to be treated like an underclass – if the black majority continues to be treated like a color cast as if we're in India or something – than what difference does it make what color the President is? If the black elite joins the white elite in oppressing working-class people both white and black I fail to see how that improves conditions for the black worker.

Q. Do you think that the election of a black President will cause or rather increase tensions in the black community along economic lines?

A. It might. At first, the election of a black President will unite the black community. But once the black majority who are suffering economically realize that changing the color of the President changes little else than the black majority is going to get mad and frustrated – and for good reason! The black nationalists, who no doubt are pushing a black President very hard in the black community, will lose clout and credibility. What both black workers and white workers need to do is forget about the Democrats and the Republicans. We need our own party – a workers party!

Q. But don't you think the Democratic nominee deserves a chance? You're already condemning him, and he hasn't even been President yet!

A. No capitalist politician either Democrat or Republican deserves a chance! These politicians, both black and white, Democrat and Republican, have gotten us into two wars at the same time, have given the rich endless tax breaks while the rest of us pay and pay endless taxes to support a huge war machine. Huge numbers of black people are behind prison bars for no other reason than drugs, and yet black people aren't any more likely to use drugs than white people. Two million Americans behind prison bars every night is just too much! We are living in a democracy in name only, it is a democracy of the rich and powerful, and the rest of us are being left out.

Q. But the fact that black people are so badly treated in this country – isn't that the reason why we need a black president?

A. The fact that black people have been so brutally oppressed for 400 years is the reason why we need a workers revolution. We live under a government that was founded by slaveholders and slave traders. Black people – or most black people excluding the black elite – will never be free as long as they live under a system founded by slaveholders and slave traders. Having a black face in a high place will change nothing for the black majority. Most black people will continue to be disproportionately poor, will continue to be incarcerated in disproportionately high rates just for being black. When Chicago had its first black mayor I remember when a couple of white cops beat up a black female bus driver with impunity. While Chicago had its first black mayor white cops beat up black men in police stations all the time! While Chicago had its first black mayor black people became poorer.

Q. But that's not the fault of the mayor. It would have been the same if the mayor had been white – right?

A. Yes. And that's exactly my point! Having black faces in high places changes nothing. The system we are living under is inherently racist. The only solution is to get rid of the racist capitalist system. We need a workers revolution.

Feminism or Women's Liberation?

An Interview with Wolf Larsen

Question: I notice that you're hostile to feminism – why is that?

Answer: I feel that feminism has betrayed the struggle for women's liberation. For the past few decades the feminists have been pushing sexual Puritanism, instead of leading the fight for women's equality. The born-again Christians are also pushing sexual Puritanism. It's just disgusting that the feminists sound like a bunch of puritanical born-again Christians, especially considering that the born-again Christians are always attacking women's rights.

Q. I see, so you don't like sexual Puritanism, and you equate feminism with sexual Puritanism – and that's why you don't like feminism?

A. Yes, that's the main reason, but not the only one.

Q. What are some of the other reasons you are hostile to feminism?

A. The feminists always seem to support the Democrats, no matter what horrible crime the Democrats have committed lately. When the last Democratic administration ended welfare as we know it and replaced it with slavefare I thought it was disgusting the way that many feminists refused to criticize the Democratic administration for this horrible thing. As you probably know most people who received welfare were poor women and their children.

Q. But feminists have contributed a lot to the struggle for women's rights – look at the women's right to vote – we can thank the feminists for that, can't we?

A. Actually, women in the Soviet Union got the right to vote a year before women in the United States got the right to vote. Perhaps the American government gave women the right to vote because here the American government was criticizing the Soviet Union for so-called totalitarianism and yet women had the right to vote there but not here in the US.

Q. But what about the struggle for equal pay for equal work?

A. Yes, I remember feminists talking about equal pay for equal work when I was a young teenager in junior high. I haven't heard them talk about equal pay for equal work very much since, and now I'm a balding middle-aged man. (Laughs) In the interim I've heard the feminists mostly talk about how evil testosterone and men are, and how sex and nudity is supposedly degrading to women.

Q. But men are evil (Laughs) – aren't they? But more seriously don't you think pornography is degrading to women?

A. Regarding your first question I've heard women in Brazil say a man is the same as a dog. That seems mean. Why would anyone say that about a dog? (Laughs) In regards to your second question no I do not believe pornography is degrading to women. If you go out of your way you might be able to find some pornography that's degrading to women. However, I can tell you from personal experience that most pornography is not degrading to women. Just because a woman is naked with her legs open in a picture – that is natural. Women have been getting naked and opening their legs ever since there were human beings! And lots of women like getting naked and opening up their legs – look at all the people on our planet – how do you think they all got here? I can't think of anything more natural than getting naked and having sex! But if someone doesn't want to get naked and have sex, well they shouldn't get naked and have sex if they don't want to, but they shouldn't try to impose their puritanical ideas on everybody else! What's oppressive to women is paying them less money for the same work. What's oppressive to women is the lack of quality affordable childcare. I think good quality child care should be free for all working women. I think the feminists are focusing on things regarding sex because they are puritanical and also because they want to distract women from what the real issues are. The real issues are equal pay for equal work, free abortion on demand, and free quality child care for all working women – which are all things I strongly support!

Q. But don't you think that pornography causes violence against women?

A. No I don't think that! That's silly! Violence against women is a serious problem – but it is not caused by pornography. Anybody who says that pornography causes violence against women obviously doesn't know much about pornography. Pornography is naked people. Pornography is people having sex. Pornography is natural. Nudity is natural. Sex is natural.

Q. But aren't there depictions of violence against women in pornography?

A. If you went out of your way you could find that. But, it's just as easy to find depictions of women being violent towards men in pornography, you know the whole dominatrix thing. In fact the latter seems to be more common than the former.

Q. So you defend pornography then?

A. Yes, of course. As long as all the people involved are adults, and everything is consensual. I think the whole anti-pornography thing, and the whole puritanical thing of the feminists, is a bunch of nonsense to distract us from the struggle for women's liberation, which begins with the struggle for equal pay for equal work, free abortion rights, and free quality child care. I'd like to touch upon a subject you mentioned before: violence against women.

Q. Go ahead.

A. Unlike the feminists and most of the other so-called progressives in our country I am a strong defender of the Second Amendment! Women should have the right to defend themselves from violent men! Men are physically more powerful than women, but the Second Amendment makes all of us male or female equal. I think women should have the right to use the Second Amendment against rapists. I think women should have the right to use the Second Amendment if they are being beaten by their boyfriends or husbands. Most feminists are against the Second Amendment, and thus the feminists condemn women to be the victims of violent men. If women don't have the right to protect themselves with the Second Amendment then who's going to protect them? The trigger-happy police? By the time the police arrive the women are often dead, or severely beaten, or raped. And when women defend themselves against violent men with the Second Amendment they are often hauled away in handcuffs as if they were criminals. This is an outrage! Women must have the right to defend themselves! The best way to stop violence against women is to give women the right to defend themselves!

Q. Do you think it's a good idea for you to criticize feminism – after all you are a man!

A. Yes I'm a man – so what! Many men have wives and girlfriends who work. If women's wages were raised to be the same as men's then there would be more money in American households – and lots of men would support that! Also, many men would support free quality child care for all working women – because that would be one less household expense – and also because everyone wants their children to receive good quality child care. Usually parents don't want their children just to be plunked in front of some television set. When I was a longshoreman my union had a strong position defending women's right to an abortion, and it would have been great if us so-called "macho" blue collar guys were called out to defend abortion clinics. I'll tell you, we'd give a new meaning to Bible thumping. We'd teach those born-again Christians to leave abortion clinics alone!

Q. Do you think feminists misrepresent men – particularly blue-collar men like yourself?

A. Well, I was a blue-collar man for 12 years. And yes I do believe that feminists misrepresent men. Some men are every rotten word you can think of. But most men are okay. Most men do not beat women. Most men do not rape women. There are many men like myself who strongly support women's struggle for liberation and equality. It's important for men to support the struggle for women's liberation and equality. I think that feminist male-bashing only divides male and female workers against each other, and the only people that serves is the bosses. Regarding blue-collar men I think we are often misrepresented on television and whatnot. We are not all ignorant. In fact, I think most blue-collar men are more intelligent than George Bush, our current president, and he went to Yale, which seriously makes me doubt the intelligence of many Ivy League graduates. (Laughs)

Q. So what do you propose as a replacement for feminism, if it's really true as you contend that feminists are not fighting for women's rights strongly enough?

A. It's not just that feminists are not fighting strongly enough for women's liberation. The problem is feminists are not fighting for women's liberation at all. I can't even remember the last time that I heard a feminist even bring up a subject remotely connected to women's rights – like equal pay for equal work, or free quality child care for all working women. The fact that the feminists ally themselves with the Democrats is truly repulsive to me – because the Democrats don't give a damn about women's rights. What we need is a third party – a workers party – a party that will fight for free abortion on demand, free contraceptives, equal pay for equal work, and free quality child care.

Q. But one of the major candidates in the Democratic primaries was a woman – how can you say that the Democrats don't care about women's rights?

A. During the last Clinton administration Hillary flew halfway across the world to lecture the Chinese on women's rights when meanwhile here in America the born-again Christians were bombing abortion clinics. Putting a woman's face in high places changes nothing for *working-class* women. If the President of the United States of America has a vagina between her legs what difference does that make for the women struggling to find quality affordable childcare for her children? What difference does it make for women struggling to pay the bills on miserly wages? (You know a woman is often paid less than a man for doing the same work!) Having a woman as President will do nothing to improve the lives of *working-class* women. To improve the lives of *working-class* women we need a workers party that will fight for the rights of working women.

Defend Immigrants! Immigrants Should Have All the Same Rights As Native-Born Citizens!

An Interview with Wolf Larsen

Question: Why do you call for full rights for immigrants? Shouldn't people born here in the United States have more rights than immigrants?

Answer: We're all human beings. We should all enjoy the same rights as human beings.

Q. When you call for equal rights for immigrants are you also speaking of the right to work?

A. Yes.

Q. But aren't immigrants stealing jobs away from Americans?

A. No, they're not. The United States has always had immigration. The United States is a country of immigrants – with the exception of the Indians the rest of us are all the descendents of immigrants. The reason that there are less jobs is because the big corporations are exporting our jobs abroad. So it's not the immigrants who are robbing jobs. The problem is that the corporations are robbing American jobs by exporting our jobs abroad. The other problem is that capitalism has always had unemployment. The bosses want unemployment so that there will be people desperate enough to take your job if you demand higher wages or better working conditions. In addition, capitalism has a boom and bust cycle that causes recessions which in turn cause large-scale unemployment. Therefore, the cause of unemployment is capitalism. The immigrants are not causing unemployment. Hence, American workers should welcome immigrants with open arms.

Q. Welcome immigrants with open arms? Why?

A. Let me give you an historical example. When black workers began migrating north they were for the most part rejected by the traditional craft unions. I'm not speaking about the industrial unions, which did not exist yet. Many of the traditional craft unions rejected black workers. They said that black workers were stealing jobs from white men. The result was that quite a few blacks crossed the picket lines of white workers. If white workers and these unions had welcomed blacks into their ranks then the labor movement in the North would have been far more united and stronger. United both the white workers and black workers would have come out the winners. But because they were divided against each other both the white workers and black workers came out the losers. I say losers because the result of white and black workers being divided against each other was lower wages for both. When industrial unions came along and united black and white workers at the workplace the result was higher wages for both. When you don't welcome your fellow workers into your ranks and unite with them then the workers will be conquered because they're divided against each other. If native-born Americans are divided against immigrant workers and vice-versa then the only people who will win from this are the bosses and the big corporations. The result of native-born workers and immigrant workers being divided against each other is lower wages. The native-born workers should fight for the rights of the immigrant workers, and that way we will all make more money.

Q. But wouldn't it be better for the American workers if the illegal immigrant workers were just deported?

A. No, it wouldn't. As long as there are employers willing to exploit them there will be plenty of illegal immigrants. For every illegal immigrant that's deported there will be another one coming to take his place. There is an endless supply of misery in Third World capitalist countries. Minimum wage in these countries are a fraction of what they are in the United States. There's so much poverty in these countries. People do almost anything to get out. Trying to stop this huge mass of desperate people from coming into our country is impossible, particularly when there's so many employers who are all too happy to exploit them. You have to look at other factors too – like corruption. Often times the immigration officials arrive at a workplace to round up these illegal immigrants on payday – just before these people were to be paid for two weeks of labor. So the best thing for American workers to do is to fight for full rights for these immigrant workers – so that way immigrate workers can demand fair wages and decent working conditions. That way the American worker is not being undermined by a group of desperate people willing to work for any kind of wages under horrible working conditions. Immigrant workers are more likely to take a militant stance for higher wages and better working conditions if they know they're not going to be deported for doing so. One of the reasons that employers don't want illegal immigrants to get their papers is because employers want to keep on exploiting them. The employers want the illegal immigrants to keep on coming. Employers want to keep on exploiting the immigrant workers. And that's why many employers don't want the immigrant workers to get their papers.

Q. Wouldn't the solution be to improve wages back in these Third World countries? So that these workers don't come here?

A. I wouldn't hold my breath waiting for that to happen. In the Third World exploitation of the worker is horrible. In many Third World countries in Latin America minimum wage is currently about a dollar an hour. In the United States minimum wage is currently about seven dollars an hour. In many of these Third World countries in Latin America when you go to the supermarket you notice that many necessary items like soap, toothpaste, toothbrush, and many food items are the same as in the United States. So the poverty is brutal. And often times the employers of these workers have a very wealthy lifestyle. Other times the employers of these workers are American corporations. So it's the very nature of the capitalist system that workers of the

Third World are so exploited and so poorly paid they will do anything to get to a first world country, where maybe they will live in poverty but at least it won't be quite as bad as in their home country. Also, it seems like often when the workers in Latin America rise up to demand better wages they are mowed down by army and police bullets. And those bullets are often made in America, they are supplied by the American government. Our own American government is helping the governments of Latin America keep their own working people down. Sometimes when these Latin American governments lose control of the situation and the people are in revolt the American military comes in and kills a lot of people. So you see when the working people in these Third World countries fight for better wages they are often shot down like flies, with bullets supplied by the American government.

Q. But hasn't government repression come to an end in Latin America now that most of Latin America's governments are democratically elected?

A. Most of the Latin American governments are democratically elected, but minimum wage in these countries or most of them is still very low and poverty is still very widespread. Regardless of whether the government is a dictatorship or democratically elected the working people go on suffering in these countries. That is why they are desperate to immigrate to the United States or any other first world country. Union leaders and strike leaders in these countries are still often shot in broad daylight. If workers try to form a union they are often still fired, as they are in the United States. And these Latin American governments are still armed usually with armaments by the American government. And Uncle Sam is always ready to step in and invade if it looks like the workers will succeed in kicking out a bourgeois government. I think we need to realize that the immigrants from Latin America and other parts of the world are fleeing desperate economic conditions, just like our own immigrant ancestors. And no matter what they're going to keep on coming, especially because employers here in the United States are more than happy to exploit them. So what we have to do is fight for the equal rights of these immigrant workers. And what's more American workers can learn a lot from these immigrant workers.

Q. Why do you say that American workers can learn a lot from immigrant workers?

A. Many workers from Latin America come from a very militant working-class history. These workers have had to fight very hard for what little rights they have. Sometimes I believe that the American worker has not been militant enough lately in defending himself against union-busting and other attacks against the workers. In addition, not that Latin America is perfect when it comes to the subject of race but compared to the United States many Latin American workers grew up in a tradition where black, white, indigenous, and mixed-race workers are all united together in a common goal of fighting together to make more money. We all want to make more money, right? The only way for all of us in the United States to make more money – is for the workers to all unite together across racial lines and whatnot and fight together for better wages and better working conditions. Black workers, white workers, straight workers, gay workers, male workers, female workers, workers born in the United States and immigrant workers must all unite together in common struggle to make more money and to fight for the right of all to have jobs. The employers and the politicians and the news media (which is owned by the employers) use the immigrant as a scapegoat for the American worker's problems. But who was it that caused the latest economic collapse? The big corporations! And the big corporations have been bailed out with the tax dollars from working people. So really, it's the big corporations and the politicians who are hurting the American worker. The employers and the politicians and the news media want to use the immigrants as scapegoats the same way that Hitler and the Nazi party used the Jews as scapegoats for the problems in Germany during the Weimer Republic era. The Jews had nothing to do with the problems in Germany during the Weimer Republic era. The Jews were just scapegoats back then the same way that the immigrants are scapegoats today. The immigrants have not caused the enormous problems that we see in the United States today. It is the big corporations and the politicians of both parties that have caused these problems. And it is important for white workers to remember that many of their own ancestors were immigrants. Back when our ancestors immigrated to this country the employers and politicians and news media treated our Irish, Italian, German, and Eastern European ancestors the same way that they are treating the predominately Latino immigrants today. When you spit on immigrants today you are spitting on your own ancestors. When you perpetrate bigoted hysteria against today's immigrants you are perpetrating the same kind of bigoted hysteria that your own immigrant ancestors were victims of. And if you think of that immigrant co-worker as being your enemy you are foolish. The employer is your enemy, not the immigrant. The employer wants to pay you as little as possible. If you have a union the employer wants to smash your union. If you don't have a union then the employer will do everything to stop you from getting one. The only way that you will get better wages and better working conditions is by uniting with all the workers around you to fight for better wages and working conditions.

It Will Take a Workers Revolution to Free Gays & Lesbians!

An Interview with Wolf Larsen

Question: Why do you say it will take a workers revolution to free gays and lesbians?

Answer: It's obvious. Both political parties are hostile to gays and lesbians! Gays and lesbians are discriminated against in every aspect of life. Even if one day the government recognizes the right of gays and lesbians to marry homosexuals will still be discriminated against in everyday life. There needs to be a fundamental huge change! We need to take this society and throw it in the garbage can and begin a new society so that everyone will be free – including gays and lesbians.

Q. I don't understand. Why do you say we need to throw our society in the garbage can?

A. The society that we live under was founded by the Puritans. It is still a thoroughly puritanical society. America is the most religious of all the first world countries. Nothing more than a great big change will make it possible for gays and lesbians to be free.

Q. I disagree. Why not reform the system to bring rights to gays and lesbians?

A. Homosexuals have been trying to reform the system for ages! It hasn't worked! Gays and lesbians are still at the margins of society. They currently don't even have the right to marry. Even if they acquire the right to marry they will still face widespread discrimination everywhere. We need a new government. A government that will not tolerate discrimination against anyone – regardless of their sexual preference, race, gender, and national origin, religion or lack of, etc. We need a government firmly committed to equality for all! When I say equality for all I don't mean we're all going to make the same money – people will be paid according to their work – when I speak of equality I mean that everyone must have the same rights and those rights must be a reality in everyday life, not just pretty words on some piece of paper.

Q. I see. But what about the Democratic Party? Won't the Democrats eventually bring about gay rights?

A. I doubt it. The Democrats haven't even brought women's rights, let alone gay rights. Look at the rotten record of the Democrats on women's issues. Democrats haven't even brought equal pay for equal work, although there was a lot of talk about that some time ago, but it was just talk and no action. Even if they passed an equal pay for equal work legislation for women the government probably wouldn't even bother enforcing it. Women don't even have free quality child care. And women's rights to an abortion are being slowly whittled away. If this society can't even bring women's equality how is this society going to bring about gay equality? In this society gays and lesbians are even more vilified than women! So if this society can't bring about women's equality I really doubt it can bring about gay equality. You have to throw capitalism in the garbage can. And that's all there is to it.

Q. You propose a workers revolution in order to throw capitalism in the garbage and build a new society. But wasn't the Soviet Union homophobic as well?

A. In the beginning the Soviet Union was very much for the rights of gays and lesbians. The Soviet Union was the first country to take anti-sodomy laws off the books. As you probably know anti-sodomy laws are used to persecute homosexuals. Anyway, the Soviet Union took the anti-sodomy laws off the books back in 1919. And now in the 21st century I understand that there are still some states in the USA that have anti-sodomy laws on the books. However, the Soviet Union became homophobic under Stalin and the Stalinist bureaucracy. Virtually all Stalinist groups are hostile to homosexuals. However, Trotskyists, on the other hand, are completely different. Trotskyists defend gay rights! Leon Trotsky led the October Revolution with Lenin. Trotskyists are the true communists. Trotskyists defend gay rights!

Q. How would a workers government treat gays and lesbians?

A. In a Trotskyist government gays and lesbians would have all the same rights as everyone else. Gays and lesbians would have the right to marry. A Trotskyist government would defend gays and lesbians against any and all forms of discrimination. A Trotskyist government would defend homosexuals against gay bashing. Gays would have the right to defend themselves with the second amendment against any violent bigots. Once there were enough violent homophobic bigots under the ground than I think society would get the message. Don't mess with gays! Discrimination against gays in employment and housing and education and everything else would not be tolerated. People who practice discrimination against gays and lesbians would be punished.

Q. That all sounds like a nice idea in theory but I don't expect there will be a workers revolution tomorrow morning. What do you propose in the meantime, I mean how do you further the cause of gay equality in the meantime before this revolution?

A. In the meantime the gays and lesbians can forget about the Democrats! The Democrats don't give a damn about gay rights! What we need is a workers party. A workers party would be a third party alternative to the Democrats and the Republicans. A workers party would fight for the rights of human beings, as opposed to fighting for the rights of animals like the Green party. A workers party would fight for the rights of gays! A workers party would fight for the rights of gays to marry and adopt children. A workers party would do whatever it could – whatever necessary – to defend gay men against these cowardly attacks from violent homophobic bigots. A workers party would do everything it could to educate working-class Americans that it is necessary to defend all workers – including gay workers. A workers party would fight against discrimination of gays in the workplace. A workers party would also fight against discrimination against gays in housing and education and everything else. It's time for gays and lesbians to forget about the Democrats. The Democrats are no different than the Republicans. The Democrats treat gays and lesbians like third class citizens! We need a workers party!

Why Young People Should Embrace Socialism

An Interview with Wolf Larsen

Question: So why should young people embrace socialism?

Answer: Why not? Socialists believe that everyone should be entitled to a free college education. Socialists believe that young people should be entitled to free job training. We also fight for the rights of veterans. We believe that all veterans should receive the medical care and benefits they need without too much bureaucratic red tape. The same politicians that blabber about supporting our troops and send young people into war are the same politicians that abandon many of our young people when they come back from the war with injuries and other medical problems.

Q. But wouldn't providing all young people with a free college education and free job training be expensive?

A. Giving our young people a free college education and free job training would be a lot less expensive than sending them into war. We are against war. We fight for peace. If there's peace then there's money for all kinds of things.

Q. What else does socialism offer young people?

A. More freedom! Today if a young person lights up of marijuana joint he runs the risk of being thrown in jail, where he might get raped. And if someone gets raped in jail they might get AIDS. Imagine that – getting AIDS for smoking a marijuana joint! It's ridiculous! The politicians talk endlessly about our freedom and democracy but yet they are the same ones that take away our freedoms. Nobody should be thrown into jail because of drugs. Young people can't even have a drink! The drinking age is 21. At 18 you can sign up and go to war and decide to put your life at risk, but you can't even have a drink! So you're free to go off to war to die, but you don't even have the freedom to order a beer at a bar! What kind of freedom is that?!

Q. But doesn't the Armed Forces offer opportunities for people who might otherwise be unemployed?

A. The reason that so many young people are unemployed and don't have any opportunities is because of capitalism. The capitalists benefit from a lot of unemployment because it makes the people who are working willing to work for less money – if they complain about their miserly wages it's easy to replace them with someone else who's desperate and unemployed. Under socialism everyone will have the right to a job. Minimum wage will be doubled. So young people will benefit enormously from having a right to a job, a right to a free college education, the right to free job training, and the right to a minimum wage that's double what it is today. And young people have historically made lower wages, so a higher minimum wage will be very beneficial to young people.

Q. But wouldn't a higher minimum wage hurt many young people – because then there would be less jobs?

A. No. Because under socialism everyone will have the right to a job.

Q. But socialism seems so stifling! I don't think young people are ready for something like that!

A. It's capitalism that's stifling! Look at AIDS. If a young person has sex without a condom they can die! I can't think of anything more stifling then the fact that if I don't wear condom I might die. Instead of putting endless money into war like under capitalism a socialist government would put lots and lots of money into a cure for things like AIDS. It's very important that people be able to have as much sex as they want without worrying about getting some deadly disease. There should also be endless free birth control options for everyone of reproductive age. That way, everyone can have as much sex as they want to with whoever they want and not worry about dying or unwanted pregnancies. Under capitalism you can die for having sex. Now that's stifling!

Q. But what many young people may like about capitalism is the idea that they can rise to the top and become a millionaire or even President of the United States! Capitalism provides opportunity for young people – isn't that true?

A. The chance that any one person will become a millionaire

or President of the United States is very slim! Capitalism dooms lots of young people to unemployment and miserly wages. You can dream all you want but the reality for many young people is that the only opportunities capitalism offers them is McDonald's or Wal-Mart. And in the capitalist third world it's even worse – far worse! In the third world there are literally masses of young people who have few choices and few opportunities in life. Capitalism stifles the vast majority of young people! It may provide limitless opportunities for a very small number of privileged youth, but the reality under capitalism for the vast majority of young people is one of suffering, a lack of opportunities, endless war, and the stifling of individual freedoms. Under capitalism young people can't even have a drink!

Q. Young people are more idealistic than older people. Perhaps many of them have more on their mind than just being able to order a drink in a bar?

A. Well, when I was 18 they raised the drinking age to 21 and they grandfathered in everybody the year before me. So I was the first generation of people in that particular state who couldn't legally have a drink till I was 21 – and that made me mad! But you're right young people do think more about what direction society should take, possibly because young people have a lot longer to live. Perhaps some older people are more conservative because many of them are just trying to get by until they die. Younger people – at least some of them – want to change the world. Many younger people see a world of poverty, war, injustice, and the stifling of freedom – just to name a few of the world's problems. Capitalism has nothing to offer future generations except more war, more poverty, more suffering, more racial hatred, more homophobia etc. Eventually, capitalism may bring about World War III and a nuclear holocaust and the extinction of the human race. The hypocrites in Washington, DC talk about rogue states acquiring nuclear weapons while the biggest warmongering rogue state in the world is the one in Washington, DC. The nuclear nuts in the White House have the biggest arsenal of nuclear weapons in the world! And that is a huge threat to the future of humanity. The only way to stop all these endless wars and bloodshed and possibly an eventual nuclear war is to throw this system of capitalism in the garbage can. Capitalism produces nothing but war. That's why we need socialism. So that humanity will not face nuclear extinction. When the entire world is socialist we will destroy nuclear weapons. And children will read about the dark ages of the human race when people couldn't get medical care because they couldn't afford it, when huge numbers of people suffered in poverty, when huge numbers of people suffered unemployment, and when the nuclear race lived under the shadow of nuclear weapons. When socialism is established in the entire world then the dark ages of humanity we are living under today will be history. It will be no more. And that's why young people should embrace socialism. So that the human race can live a decent life with decent wages, the right to a job, the right to decent affordable housing, etc.

Q. Okay. Now I thinking you're sounding too idealistic. You're talking about some workers paradise.

A. What workers paradise? Workers must rule – because working-class people built this country – working-class people built the world! It's the labor of workers that makes everything possible – and that's why workers must rule. The rich people have been running the show up till now and look at the horrible state the world is in! I'm not talking about a workers paradise. I'm talking about socialism – a society where everyone has the right to a job, and where young people are not burdened by huge amounts of college debt. There will not be any college debt because college will be free. Job training will be free. Under socialism it will be easier for the vast majority of ambitious young people to advance towards their goal of living a better life. Because they will have the tools to do so, like a free college education and free job training. Plus you'll be able to have a beer, smoke a joint without worrying about going to jail, and be able to have sex without worrying about dying because a socialist government will do everything it can to find a cure for AIDS. Capitalism offers the human race nothing but endless suffering. Socialism will provide a decent standard of living for all.

Why Older People Should Embrace Socialism

An Interview with Wolf Larsen

Question: So why should older people embrace socialism?

Answer: There's lots of reasons. First of all medical care and medicine will be free under socialism. Free medical care and medicine will be a human right under socialism. Second of all a decent pension will also be a fundamental human right under socialism. Older people have worked their whole lives and they should have the right to retire with a decent standard of living. Nobody should have to work in their old age just to get by! If someone wants to work in their old age it should be a personal choice, it shouldn't be forced upon them by economic circumstances. I think another major benefit of socialism for older people is knowing that their children, their grandchildren, and the great-grandchildren and all of their descendents will live in a better world.

Q. Why do you say that the descendents of older people will live a better life under socialism?

A. Because under capitalism much of humanity is doomed to poverty, inadequate medical care, and endless war. Under socialism everyone will have the right to quality free medical care. Everyone will have the right to a job at a decent wage. Everyone will have the right to decent housing and there will be no more war.

Q. What else can socialism offer to older people?

A. More attention has to be given to improving the lives of older people. There should be more centers for senior citizens, and these centers should offer lots of fun activities for senior citizens. In such places and activities seniors can meet other seniors. Who knows, maybe socialism will even improve their sex lives!

Q. (Laughs) Socialism will improve the sex lives of senior citizens?

A. Why not? If there's more quality senior citizen centers for older people with more activities for older people than older people can meet each other and have all the sex they want! Plus under socialism Viagra and all other medications will be free. Under socialism the government will do everything it can to reach a cure for AIDS. So we can eliminate the element of fear in sex. Also, free medical care and medicines will make seniors healthier, and that will make sex better than ever!

Q. But there's already Viagra. Isn't that enough? (Laughs)

A. Viagra is a start. Under socialism there will be a greater commitment to improving the lives of senior citizens. Pharmaceutical companies will be nationalized – so that the pharmaceutical industry under socialism will put people's health before profits. Sex enhancing drugs that don't affect one's health by raising one's blood pressure would be just one way that a system committed to improving the lives of senior citizens could make things better for senior citizens.

Q. Okay, let's move on – what else can socialism do for senior citizens?

A. Socialism will make the streets safer. Everyone will have the right to a job with decent wages. Hence, there will be less muggings. Since my own grandmother was killed by a mugger I feel rather strongly about this. Senior citizens will have the right to defend themselves with the Second Amendment, so it will be hazardous to one's health to mess with senior citizens! I think that there would have to be measures taken to make things like public transportation and everything else more accessible to seniors.

Q. Isn't public transportation already accessible to seniors?

A. When it gets crowded public transportation can be dangerous for some senior citizens. Sometimes the rolling motions of buses throw senior citizens about, and they can get injured! Under socialism it will be very important to educate the rest of the population about some of the particular ways that we can make life safer for senior citizens. Whatever it takes so that seniors can travel safely on public transportation must be done. No one should be stuck at home. Whether it's public transportation or something else, everything should be done to make the life of senior citizens better. Unfortunately, under capitalism the needs of senior citizens and just about everybody else is secondary to corporate profits. Socialism – on the other hand – puts people first. And after working their entire lives senior citizens deserve better than what they're getting today under capitalism.

Q. What about housing?

A. Seniors must have the right to quality and accessible housing. Under socialism no greedy landlord will be able to excessively raise the rent on some senior citizen on a fixed income. Under socialism, no senior citizen will go homeless or hungry. Basic services like heat and electricity will be a right for seniors. After all, seniors have been working their whole lives – they've earned it!

Q. What would the socialists do about nursing homes?

A. When one thinks of nursing homes today lots of negative images come to mind. It doesn't have to be that way! If and when the day comes that a person can't take care of themselves or needs help that they can't get at home and they need to be in a nursing home well then a nursing home should be a quality living environment. Older people shouldn't just be dumped in substandard nursing homes to die! Nursing homes should be a quality environment, and if that means changing them completely then let's do it! Resources must be spent so that older people live the last years of their lives with dignity, with as little suffering is possible. The last years of one's life should be fun! People who worked their whole lives deserve a better old age than they're getting today! Many senior citizens around the world have it difficult today – certainly not all – but many. That's the reality under capitalism. That's why we need socialism.

Why Should Small Business Owners Support Socialism?

An Interview with Wolf Larsen

Question: So why should small business owners support socialism?

Answer: Under capitalism big corporations are constantly putting so many small businesses out of business.

Q. But isn't that just the way the market is? Perhaps big corporations are more efficient than small business, and that's why big corporations push out smaller businesses?

A. In some cases that may be true. However, in other cases it may be that the big corporations engage in unfair practices – and then small businesses go under.

Q. I thought that socialists were hostile to business. Under socialism will there be small businesses?

A. Of course there will be small businesses under socialism! Particularly if Trotskyists are in power. I'm not so sure about the Stalinists, many of them have weird ideas. But Trotskyists believe in helping small business. And under socialism small businesses won't need to worry about being pushed out of business by big corporations because there will be no big corporations – under socialism all the major corporations will be nationalized.

Q. Under socialism will smaller businesses be nationalized too?

A. Certainly not. Only major industries like steel, automobiles, airplanes and banking will be nationalized. Socialists believe that small business has an important role to play in the economy, and that small business should be encouraged. Under socialism small businesses will qualify for low-interest loans. Under capitalism – in contrast – banks often do not want to give out loans to small businesses. Under capitalism interest rates go up and down like crazy, and often interest rates are ridiculously high.

Q. But won't socialism hurt entrepreneurship?

A. On the contrary socialism will be good for entrepreneurship. Socialism will encourage entrepreneurship. Under socialism like I said there will be low-interest loans available to small businesses. If a person has a dream of opening up a small business they won't need to worry about being squashed by big corporations because there won't be any big corporations. Big corporations are the enemy of entrepreneurship. In addition, the general population will have more time and money to spend in small businesses. Minimum wage will be doubled. Everyone will have the right to a job. Workers will have the 30 hour work week. Affordable quality housing will be a right, as will free quality child care and free quality medical care. As a result, the majority of the population will have more free time and more disposable income than ever before. That will be great for the bottom line of small businesses! In addition, the boom and bust cycle of capitalism with its horrible recessions will be history. Under socialism the economy will be far less erratic. And that will be great for small businesses – because all these recessions under capitalism force many small businesses to close.

Q. But what if a small business person becomes rich? What will happen to them under socialism?

A. Under capitalism most small business people work hard but they never become rich. People open small businesses for various reasons, but a common reason is that some people want to be their own boss. However, the reality is under capitalism the vast majority of small business people never become rich. They work hard. They get by. Under socialism the majority of small business people will be better off than they were under capitalism. However, it's impossible to make everyone happy all the time. Under socialism there will be no multimillionaires. For example, let me explain a scenario that could very well happen under socialism. If someone owns many many McDonald's franchises then that person will lose all but one of their McDonald's franchises without compensation. (Billionaires & multimillionaires will not be entitled to compensation for seized businesses under socialism.) Anyway, if the Socialist government doesn't want to be bothered with the McDonalds restaurants then the rest of the McDonald's franchises would be distributed to others. Socialism will destroy the big businessmen and that will create many opportunities for small businesses.

Q. Why would a socialist government distribute those franchises to others?

A. Number one to create more small business people, which is good. And number two a socialist government will not be able to trust multimillionaires. In the past multimillionaires have financed counterrevolutionary movements that have caused the lives of so many workers. The fact is multimillionaires are a threat to both workers and most small business people. Multimillionaires would most likely want to bring back capitalism, and they might finance violent counterrevolutionary movements. In order to prevent that kind of bloodshed and chaos a socialist government would have to make sure that there would be no multimillionaires.

Q. But don't you think a change from capitalism to socialism could put some small businesses out of business?

A. That's possible. But I think that the change from capitalism to socialism would be beneficial to most small businesses. In addition, a socialist government would help out small businesses with low-interest loans that would help them make whatever changes necessary to be prosperous in a socialist society.

Q. What about the professionals? What will happen to the professionals under socialism?

A. It depends on the profession. Remember, under socialism you're paid according to your work. For example, a doctor will make more than a clerk, because being a doctor is a very important skill. However, everyone will make a decent wage.

Q. But I still think that socialism would hurt innovation and therefore hurt small business.

A. On the contrary the opposite will happen. More people will have more money than ever before and there will be more prosperity and leisure time than ever before so that people will have more time and more money to spend in small businesses. Right now the corporations are crowding out small businesses left and right. Landlords often prefer to rent a storefront out to the branch of some big corporation then to some small business. For this reason and many others it is often difficult for small businesses to survive under capitalism. Small business will thrive under socialism.

Free Love Versus Religious Puritanism

An Interview with Wolf Larsen

Question: So what are your opinions regarding sex?

Answer: I think sex is natural! I think most cultures in the world are way too uptight about sex! American culture in particular is especially puritanical.

Q. Some people say that it's the other way around – that things are too permissive – particularly in America! How do you answer that?

A. I think there's a lot of hypocrisy regarding sex. They use sex to sell everything – from toothpaste to automobiles! However, you can't show people on television having sex – why not? We're not allowed to show people about safe sex on television – to show people how to correctly put on the condom for women or the condom for men. And they're not teaching many young people a good sex education in our schools, instead they teach them about abstinence. And as a result our young people are getting pregnant in huge numbers – and they're getting sexually transmitted diseases in huge numbers too.

Q. But don't you think it's the permissive nature of American society that results in so many teenagers getting STDs and pregnant?

A. American society is not permissive – American society is too puritanical! United States is the most religious and the most puritanical of all the first world countries – which is the reason why the United States has the highest teenage pregnancy rate and the highest teenage STD rates.

Q. Are you accusing the born-again Christians of causing teenage pregnancy and STDs in our country?

A. I'm not accusing the born-again Christians who actually practice Christianity of anything. However, as for the religious fanatics who are trying to enforce their puritanical hypocrisy on everybody else – yes I think they're partly responsible for all the teenage pregnancies and STDs in our country. These religious fanatics are interfering with our schools and preventing us from teaching our young people about sex. If it wasn't for these religious fanatics and rotten politicians we could teach our young people about condoms and everything else about sexuality.

Q. But if we teach our young people about sex than they might actually have sex – isn't that true?

A. Young people are already having sex! In some northern European countries they begin sexual education classes at the age of 12 – and their sexual education classes are better than those in America – because they actually teach young people something about sex! In the United States sexual education classes generally start later, and often you don't learn very much useful information except perhaps a bunch of puritanical gobbledygook about abstinence. As a result American young people are not as educated about sex and so they are getting pregnant and infected with sexually transmitted diseases in higher numbers than other industrialized countries. By the way, in many northern European countries the young people are no more likely to have sex than the young people in America – the percentage of sexually active teenagers is the same in both northern Europe and in the United States – and they began having sex at around the same age too – the difference is that northern European teenagers don't get pregnant as often and they don't get sexually transmitted diseases as often because their educational systems actually teach the young people more about sex. So yes I think we can thank the religious fanatics and their interference in our educational system for the fact that there are more pregnancies and sexually transmitted diseases amongst teenagers in our country.

Q. Don't you think a lot of religious fanatics would be flabbergasted by such an accusation?

A. Probably. (Laughs) And maybe I should be scared. The religious fanatics in our country often resort to violence when they disagree with others about something. This is actually contrary to what the New Testament teaches. The New Testament tells Christians not to resort to violence. The New Testament also tells Christians not to interfere in the government, and not to try to enforce their view of things upon others. The New Testament says you can preach to the willing, but you shouldn't try to force your opinion on everybody else. I think it's disgusting the way these religious fanatics are trying to enforce their views on sexuality and everything else upon the rest of us. And when they do so they are actually violating the teachings of the New Testament. I don't hate all Christians, I only hate the ones that try to enforce their puritanical views on the rest of us. Let me emphasize again that I have no problem with Christians that actually practice Christianity. But I can't stand the Christians who are puritanical hypocrites. They want to enforce their puritanical hypocrisy on everybody else.

Q. So you think that American society is too sexually puritanical – and that the religious fanatics are responsible for this?

A. Yes. I also blame the politicians too. The politicians – most of them – sound like a bunch of religious fanatics when it comes to the subject of sexuality. I think that's true for both Republicans and the Democrats. Bill Clinton, the last Democrat in the White House, fired the Surgeon General for suggesting that masturbation should be discussed in sexual education in schools. So I don't know why the so-called left types and liberals say it's just the Republicans that are uptight about sexuality.

Q. Why do you think the politicians act like that – is it because they want votes?

A. Of course they want votes! But it also goes to the core

values of our politicians – many of whom are either born-again Christians or devout Catholics. They seem to feel that war – and killing scores of innocent civilians – is morally acceptable. But sex is not. And teaching our young people about sex is not permissible according to many of these politicians. These politicians make it illegal for a young person of 18 to have a drink, but they can sign up and go to war and be given orders to kill people. I think these politicians are sick – both Democrat and Republican.

Q. But perhaps the politicians are just doing what people want them to do?

A. If the politicians are going to do what the people want them to do then why don't these politicians stop all these wars! Most of the American people are sick and tired of all these wars! Most of the American people want our children to receive a good solid education about sexuality – and everything else for that matter. Polls show that.

Q. But perhaps the politicians are trying to represent core American values?

A. Maybe. Core American values like Puritanism! The English couldn't stand the Puritans so they kicked them out of England and sent them here to die. Everyone else who tried to found New England before them died, but unfortunately some Indians taught the Puritans how to survive, so now these Puritans are still with us today and trying to tell us how to live our lives.

Q. So what do you believe is a healthy sexuality?

A. First of all we need to understand that sex is natural, in both adults and adolescents. Instead of spending hundreds of billions of dollars on the military we should be spending more money coming up with a cure for AIDS and genital herpes. Genital herpes by the way affects one out of every six adult Americans. We should put free condom dispensing machines on every street corner in the nation. Actually, there should be free condom dispensing machines on every streetcorner in the world!

Q. But a lot of people would object to that – they would say that would be immoral.

A. These moral types would do better to actually practice what they preach. Many of these moral types go out whoring, drugging, & drinking on Saturday night and then on Sunday morning they pretend they're a bunch of angels as they sit in church. These moral types should stop interfering in the lives of others! AIDS is not a moral crisis, it is a health crisis, and it has reached such epidemic proportions because of the irresponsible behavior of politicians.

Q. Don't you think that AIDS is caused by the irresponsible behavior of individuals, rather than politicians?

A. The reason we don't have a cure for AIDS is because the political system doesn't care about the people dying, and the political system blames the victims themselves, rather than coming up with a cure. The political system that we live under is not coming up with a cure for AIDS because they'd rather spend endless amounts of money on war rather than coming up with a cure for AIDS. So yes I do blame the politicians for the fact that there is no cure for AIDS, and I blame the religious fanatics for the kind of puritanical sexuality that permeates our society. If we lived in a society with a healthy sexuality we would have devoted the necessary resources to coming up for a cure for AIDS, rather than blaming the AIDS victims themselves, which is what many religious fanatics do. Also, I think the bourgeoisie push religion as a means of controlling the population.

Q. Many people with AIDS do not like to be referred to his victims – haven't you heard that?

A. The people dying of AIDS *are* victims – they are victims of a puritanical political system that spends too much money on war and not enough money coming up with a cure for AIDS. People with AIDS are treated poorly by our government because this puritanical society vilifies those who have sex.

Q. But if everyone only had sex with their spouse don't you think there would be a lot less sex – I mean AIDS?

A. (Laughs) Interesting faux pas! If everybody only had sex with their spouse there probably wouldn't be much sex! (Laughs) The reality is many people get bored of having sex with the same person all the time. People have desire! People want sex! It's not natural to suppress sexual desire! Everybody should have sex!

Q. But that's what many people like about Christianity – it provides a framework for people to live a disciplined life – if people were more disciplined about their behavior perhaps there would be less AIDS?

A. People are human beings – not computers. Computers are inanimate objects and are therefore more disciplined. Expecting everyone to only have boring sex with the same person their whole life is like expecting a wolf not to eat sheep. Christianity is not a realistic way to live – one can't help but notice that most Christians don't even live according to Christianity. So if these Christians can't even live according to Christianity why do they expect the rest of us to act like we're not filled with sexual desires? If some Christian wants to be a saint let them go ahead and try, but he shouldn't try to enforce his Puritanism on others.

Q. So you believe that sex is a positive thing?

A. Of course I believe sex is a positive thing! Sex alleviates tension! Sex is good for health – both mental and physical! Sex is a form of exercise! People enjoy it – they enjoy it a lot! I think everybody should have as much sex as possible!

Q. But isn't that immoral?

A. I think the problem is the so-called morality of our puritanical Christian society. Why is it moral to kill people in all these endless wars? Why is it moral to put millions of Americans behind prison bars for using or selling drugs? Why is it moral to deny medical care to people because they can't afford it? But yet if someone puts their penis in someone's pussy – and it's mutual consent – than what's immoral about that? I think it's immoral not to spend billions of dollars to come up with a cure for AIDS when people are dying! I think it's immoral not to teach our young people about sexuality! I think it's immoral to try and stop people from having sex!

Q. Why do you think it's immoral to try and stop people from having sex?

A. Because then you're interfering with a fundamental right – a fundamental human right – the right to have sex.

Q. You believe that people should have the right to have sex? You believe that having sex is a fundamental human right?

A. Yes I do! Sex is one of our biggest desires! Sex is one of our biggest needs! Some people may have to pay for sex – that's just reality – while I feel sorry for them I defend their right to do so.

Q. So you think prostitution should be legalized?

A. Definitely! But I think it should be restricted to certain areas. Like Park Avenue on the Upper East Side of New York might as well be a prostitution permitted zone since quite a few women who live there are already prostitutes – they married for money. (Laughs)

Q. Do you think teenagers should be permitted to have sex as well?

A. Why not? They're already having sex anyway! It's natural for teenagers to have sex. The age of consent should be lowered everywhere across the world to the age of puberty.

Q. But many cultures are more conservative than our puritanical born-again Christian culture, as you call it. Do you think the world is ready for that kind of thing?

A. Not everyone would like it. But so what? The people against lowering the age of consent to the age of puberty are a bunch of prudes who are not being realistic. Teenagers are not innocent. They are no more innocent than adults.

Q. But teenagers are not yet adults – do you think they're mature enough to have sex?

A. Regardless of whether they're mature or not they're already having sex! Anyway, with that kind of argument you might as well say that the 70 year olds are not mature enough to have sex! (Laughs)

Q. What do you mean by that?

A. Everybody gets passionate and carried away with sex – because it feels so good! The solution isn't to try and tell people not to have sex – because they just have sex anyway. What we need to do is have endless forms of birth control. We need to make huge improvements in birth control! There should be a vast aisle of birth control options in every supermarket in the world! Endless affordable practical birth control possibilities that don't mess with one's hormones, that come with less side effects, and that don't interfere with the pleasure of having sex. If we spent more money on birth control research and less money on war research trust me we would have endless birth control options. And pharmacies need to stop keeping birth control under lock

& key. Why is it that we have endless brands of toilet paper – endless options to wipe our asses with but not endless options of birth control? Obviously something is wrong with our society! Obviously something is wrong with this society when there are only two political parties that matter – and both parties are very puritanical and anti-sex. The problem with American society is that there's too much killing and not enough fucking.

Q. Do you think that's appropriate language?

A. What, fucking? I can't think of anything more natural than fucking! I think fucking is a beautiful word! One of the most beautiful words in the English language is not even in the dictionary! (Laughs) But that's part of the puritanical society we live in.

Q. But what about the children? Children might come across that word – shouldn't we protect the children?

A. And so what if children come across the word fucking? If they find out what the word means then they'll know how they came to exist! I think it's absolutely preposterous to try and hide the reality of sex from children. How can you hide something as gigantic and huge as sex?

Q. But aren't you concerned that children might become interested in sex?

A. Obviously you were never a child, or you have a bad memory, because children are already curious about sex. I was a child once. As a child I was curious about sex. So were all the other kids. But because I was a child I was too shy to do anything about it. Childhood sexuality is different than adolescent sexuality. Once puberty begins, forget it! Adolescents are going to have sex – and nothing that adults do is gonna change that. Before puberty children might be *curious* about sexuality, but most of them are not going to have sex. Children might play "doctor" with each other, but that's just to find out what the other gender has down there. They're curious. But they usually don't want to have sex. Children are different than teenagers, and teenagers are not children.

Q. So you don't support children having sex?

A. Of course not! I don't think we need to worry about children having sex – most children are not interested in having sex. I think there's too much hysteria about the subject. The politicians talk about oh we need to save the children and all that! The politicians create a bunch of hysteria about saving children from sex when really we should be saving children from poverty. But the politicians don't want to save children from poverty. Because the politicians represent the rich. So instead of saving our children from poverty, so instead of providing all our children with quality education, so instead of making sure that children eat safe food that doesn't have a bunch of chemicals and growth hormones the politicians – instead of saving the children from these problems the politicians create a bunch of hysteria of saving the children from pedophiles and whatnot. Not that pedophiles aren't a problem – they are. But much bigger problems are that so many children are growing up in poverty, without a decent education, without decent opportunities, etc. You have to keep it all in perspective and not get hysterical.

Q. Okay. Let's go on to some other issues I wanted to discuss. I notice that you're 40 years old and not married – you're not big on marriage – is that true?

A. The problem with marriage is that the sex gets boring! Maybe not for all couples but for many couples sex gets boring after a while. Anyway, what I do with my own personal life is my own business.

Q. But sex without marriage is immoral – isn't it?

A. No it's not. Once again, killing innocent people in all these endless wars is immoral! Corporate executives running corporations like GM into the ground and then giving themselves multimillion dollar bonuses is immoral! Corporate executives in the health insurance industry making huge profits off of denying people medical care is immoral! Throwing people in jail for smoking or selling marijuana is immoral! There is nothing immoral about consenting adults having sex with anybody they damn well please!

Q. Do you think that homosexuality is normal?

A. Of course homosexuality is normal! Homosexuality, bisexuality, experimental sex with the same gender just for the hell of it to experiment – why not? Homosexuality is completely natural! And a lot of the politicians, preachers, and priests that criticize homosexuality do it themselves!

Q. What do you think of the pedophile priests in the USA?

A. They should be given a fair trial. And if they're guilty they belong in jail. Many people say that because these priests are supposed to live a life without sex that this causes them to become sick in the head, and do these horrible things. I don't know. I'm no expert. But if they're guilty of these horrible things they belong in jail. But also let me say that pedophile-ism is when an adult has sex with someone who has not entered puberty. If an adult has consensual sex with a teenager then that is not what I consider to be pedophile-ism. Pedophile-ism – did I just make up a word? Good! We have 50 different states and 50 different ages of consent – which is insane! The age of consent should be somewhere around puberty. Pedophile-ism is when an adult has sex with a child, and teenagers are not innocent children. There's a big difference between a 14-year-old and a seven-year-old, and any law that doesn't recognize that is a bad law that should be abolished.

Q. How do you believe society should deal with sex?

A. Capitalism is not capable of dealing with sexuality in a rational manner. In a socialist society sexuality would be dealt with very differently. All resources necessary would be devoted to coming up with a cure for AIDS and genital herpes right away. There would be inoculations against sexually transmitted diseases if possible – so that nobody would have to worry about these things. Any new sexual transmitted diseases that came along would be thoroughly investigated right away and ample resources would always be devoted to coming up with a cure as soon as possible.

Q. What I mean is, how would sexuality be dealt with on a daily basis?

A. In an ideal society sex would be treated as a natural part of life. Anybody above the age of puberty could have sex with anybody they wanted to as long as there was mutual consent. People could join orgies if they wanted to. If someone didn't like the idea of orgies they could just avoid them. People would have endless forms of convenient safe birth control to choose from so that they wouldn't have babies if they didn't want them, or they could choose when they would have babies. Personally, I believe that when society has matured to the point that religious extremism has faded away than people will have healthy feelings toward sexuality. It's important to respect people's right to their religion and their centers of worship – so long as they don't try to enforce their beliefs on others.

Q. Really, you think the day will come when religious extremism has faded away ?

A. That day is a long way off. But yes I do believe the day will come when religious extremism has faded away.

Q. How would that happen – that religious extremism fades away?

A. Yes the day will come. It's a question of living in a society where everyone has the right to a job, where everyone has the right to free quality medical care, and everyone has the right to a decent pension and decent wages, and rent is affordable – that way you eliminate uncertainty and worry in people's lives. In societies where there was a workers state – like the ex-Soviet Union – religious extremism went down when people didn't need to worry about their basic necessities. People's necessities were taken care of. Also, another thing that helps religious extremism is superstition and ignorance. Improve education and the people will be less religious. There's a number of factors which will contribute to the downfall of religious extremism as society changes. But I do defend the right of people to believe in God if they so choose, and I am a strong defender of people's right to worship as they choose as long as it doesn't interfere with others, just as I'm a strong defender of people's right not to worship any so called God. In a socialist society there were be a true separation of church and state. Sexual education and evolution will be taught in the schools. You can go to church all you want. But there will be no religion in schools, religion will stay in the churches, and religious extremists will not be permitted to enforce their beliefs on others. Under socialism priests and preachers will avoid politics, and keep their sermons to the subject of religion. Christians who actually live according to the teachings of the New Testament will not have any problems under socialism. No one will have the right to enforce their religious views on others or upon society as a whole. Anyway, people talk about heaven. I think heaven is a place you can find in the bedroom. (Laughs) You're free to disagree with me, where you think heaven is is your own business.

What's Wrong with the Healthcare System?

An Interview with Wolf Larsen

Question: So what's wrong with the healthcare system?

Answer: God, where do I start? The biggest problem with the healthcare system is that it's all about money. Health care for profit is a contradiction, healthcare for profit is an oxymoron. Sure, a small number of elite people get excellent quality medical care because they have lots of money. But the rest of us have to make do with rationed health care.

Q. What do you think of health insurance companies and HMOs?

A. I think they're a bunch of Mafia. The CEOs of these HMOs and health insurance companies are becoming billionaires by denying people health care. The less medical care they deliver the more money insurance companies and HMOs make.

Q. So what should be done about health insurance and HMOs?

A. Get rid of them. If you need an operation that should be between your doctor and you. Some corporate bureaucrat shouldn't decide whether you get a lifesaving operation or not. The bureaucrat is not concerned about your health. All the corporate bureaucrat is concerned about is the insurance company's or the HMO's bottom line. Your health care should be between you and your doctor. Your healthcare should not involve corporate bureaucrats who look for excuses to deny you medical care.

Q. So with what would you replace the health-insurance companies and HMOs?

A. I would replace them all with quality medical care for all. If you need to see a doctor you see a doctor. If you need an operation you get an operation. If you need to see a specialist you see a specialist. Take all the bureaucrats out of the process. Corporate bureaucrats shouldn't be able to decide whether you get a life-saving operation are not.

Q. But isn't that socialism or communism?

A. That's right! That's what it is. In order to have free quality medical care for all we're going to have to have socialism. We're going to have to get rid of capitalism. Because capitalism is all about denying people medical care so that the insurance companies and HMOs can make a handsome profit.

Q. Why should we give people free quality medical care?

A. Because free quality medical care should be a basic human right. Everyone who works should receive free quality medical care because they pay taxes. Under capitalism you pay taxes to keep lots of people in jail, you pay taxes for endless wars, you pay taxes for a police state with two million people behind prison bars. Instead of spending money on war and warehousing huge numbers of people behind prison bars for smoking marijuana we should provide everyone with free quality medical care. There is another advantage of giving everyone free quality medical care. Instead of having like a zillion bureaucrats for every doctor you have a lot more doctors.

Q. But if we provide everyone with free medical care there will be huge lines at the clinics and hospitals and there won't be enough medical care to go around – isn't that true? And people will have to wait for months to see a specialist – isn't that true?

A. We will need to train a lot more doctors, specialists, and nurses! And going to medical school or nursing school should be free. People should be accepted to medical school based on their abilities to become excellent doctors and not on their ability to pay tuition. We need the best people to become doctors and nurses, regardless of whether they can pay for medical school or not. And also we need to build hospitals, not close them. Under capitalism they keep closing hospitals. They close hospitals and build prisons.

Q. Wouldn't providing free quality medical care for everyone be very expensive?

A. Not really. Because all the HMOs and insurance companies that are sucking money out of the medical system would be gone. All the parasites would be out of the medical system. There should only be bureaucrats to check the *quality* of medical care, as opposed to ten million bureaucrats deciding who gets medical care and who doesn't. Right now you have an endless number of bureaucrats rationing medical care. Fire most of the bureaucrats and train more doctors and nurses. It's simple. Less bureaucrats. More doctors and nurses.

Q. I still think providing free medical care for everyone would be more expensive than the existing system – don't you think so?

A. I doubt it. But we also have to define our priorities. Do we want to spend lots of money on war and warehousing huge numbers of people in prison for smoking marijuana or do we want to spend more money on health care, education, and things like that? Under capitalism there's always war. And the war budget is just devouring money – endless amounts of money. The so-called war on drugs is also devouring huge amounts of money. We need to get rid of capitalism, and replace it with a system where everyone gets free quality medical care.

Q. But what do we do until we get rid of capitalism?

A. We fight for free quality medical care for everyone. The way we do this is we break with the Democrats and the Republicans and we form a workers party. A workers party will fight for free quality medical care for everyone. Working people are very powerful. Working people don't realize all the power that they have. Working people white and black and Latino, native born and immigrant, male and female, gay and straight, should all be united in fighting together for free medical care for everyone. But we certainly won't get free medical care for all without fighting for it.

Q. But some of the Democratic politicians are proposing universal health coverage. Won't that solve the problem with our medical system?

A. No it won't. What the Democrats are proposing is universal health insurance. All that means is more bureaucrats. Many times the health insurance companies refuse to pay all of our medical bills. Often health insurance companies deny medical procedures that people need. Providing universal health insurance coverage is great for the insurance companies. It will put more bureaucrats on the payroll, and that will be great for the CEOs of insurance companies. What universal health insurance will not do is provide free quality medical care for everyone. Universal health insurance will just bring more bureaucracy. We need free quality medical care for all, not endless insurance bureaucracy.

Q. But if we provide free quality medical care for everyone won't there be people abusing the system?

A. I don't think so. Nobody wants to go to the hospital. Nobody wants an operation unless it's cosmetic. Nobody wants to go to the dentist and have a drill stuck in their mouth. This is one thing you don't need to worry about people abusing. Now on the other hand if we decided to have a program giving out free beer that would be different. (Laughs)

Q. So cosmetic surgery wouldn't be covered under free quality medical care?

A. Unless someone got into a disfiguring accident than no – cosmetic surgery would not be covered under free quality medical care for all. If you're ugly and you want cosmetic surgery well that's your problem and you have to pay for it yourself. (Laughs) But if someone got into an accident and they were disfigured – particularly in the face – then I think free quality medical care should cover that. If a child is born with a cosmetic disfigurement that would make life difficult for him – especially if the disfigurement was in the face – then I think free medical care should cover that.

Q. But don't you think that capitalism delivers good quality medical care?

A. Absolutely not. There's waiting rooms filled with people waiting endless hours to see a doctor. All over the world there is just endless people waiting in endless long lines to see a doctor.

Q. All over the world? You've experienced medical care in other countries?

A. Yes I have. Mostly in the Third World. I had an operation done in a third world country because I couldn't afford to have it done in the US. The operation didn't turn out very well. Anyway, in Third World hospitals I've seen some pretty crazy things. Unsanitary conditions. Endless people waiting endless hours for medical care. And that's in private hospitals and clinics. In the public hospitals in both the

United States and in Third World countries the waits are even longer. There are many doctors all over the world that are very committed to their work. But a lot of times all you get is just a little bit of the doctor's time after a long wait. A doctor is in such a hurry to get to all the other patients waiting to see him that a lot of times the doctors don't take the time to tell you everything that you need to know. This can have fatal consequences, or it least it may compromise your recovery from your medical problem.

Q. But don't your experiences in Third World countries prove that we should keep the medical system the way it is?

A. Quite the contrary is true. Americans are flying to Third World countries to get medical procedures and operations because they can't afford to get medical care in their own country. Often, the insurance company won't pay for an operation they need. That's ridiculous! You have the richest people in the world flying to America for their medical care, and you have Americans flying to Third World countries for their medical care because they can't afford medical care in their own country. At any rate, medical care in America is not all that good for the vast majority of Americans. It might be good for someone with lots of money. But as I said before the rest of us are getting rationed medical care. Let me take this time to move beyond America. I think everyone on this planet who works deserves free quality medical care, and everyone who wants to work should have the right to a job. So basically everyone in the world should have the right to free quality medical care.

Q. But how are Third World countries going to afford that – free quality medical care for all their citizens?

A. In some ways Third World countries have many similarities with United States. Many Third World countries are spending lots of money on their militaries. There's also lots of corruption in many Third World countries. There's lots of money there that could be used for free quality medical care and for other things like education. There are some Third World countries that are too poor to provide the people with free quality medical care for all. After workers revolution occurs across the world it will be the responsibility of the first world socialist countries to aid the poorest of the Third World countries in providing free quality medical care for their citizens until they're able to afford to do it themselves.

Q. In some countries in Western Europe with free health care don't they pay lots of taxes?

A. Not all of the tax money in those countries is going to things like education and health care. Those countries also have militaries. They may not be spending as much as the United States on their militaries, but they're still spending on military. It would be interesting to see where that tax money is going to. Under socialism everyone will be contributing to the wealth of society because everyone will have the right to a job, and thus there will be less taxes and thus there will be plenty of money for free quality medical care for all without big taxes. Capitalism is very wasteful of resources. Get rid of capitalism and provide free quality medical care for all.

Q. Don't public hospitals already provide medical care for the poor?

A. I went to a public hospital in United States over and over again trying in vain to get medical care. Many other people have had similar experiences with public hospitals. Perhaps public hospitals will attend to you if you're dying. However, what often happens is that poor people can't get the medical care that they need for health problems until those health problems become very serious. Poor people often return again and again to some public hospital or public clinic trying to get treatment for a medical condition that's minor. But since there's limited resources minor medical conditions often don't get treated and poor patients are turned away from those public hospitals and clinics without medical care. As a result their minor medical conditions become worse and later that poor person is in the emergency room with a life-threatening condition and needs an operation right away. This is bad for the medical system as a whole, and it actually increases the costs of medical care. It also is bad for the poor people themselves. And maybe I shouldn't call these people poor, because many of them have jobs, but they can't afford to pay their rent, the groceries, *and* the medical bills. Medical care is just too expensive because the system is based on a profit system that's dysfunctional. Public hospitals in Third World countries so far in my experience have been better than public hospitals in the United States – which is mind boggling. They were better because you actually got medical care. The US spends huge amounts of money on its war machine, so there's not much left over for healthcare.

Capitalism Sucks!

An Interview with Wolf Larsen

Question: Why do you say our government treats workers like dirt?

Answer: Look at minimum wage, for example. It's too difficult to survive on minimum wage in much of the United States, let alone raise a family!

Q. But the Democrats just raised minimum wage – isn't that better than nothing?

A. I'd like to see these Democrat politicians try and live on minimum wage. And I'd like to see Republican politicians try and live on minimum wage too. I doubt they could do it! Another problem with the Democrats is that they are against working-class people just like the Republicans.

Q. Really? Many people don't think so. Many people think that the Democrats are more for the workers.

A. The Democrats pretend to be the friends of workers. During election campaigns the Democrats like to put on hardhats and pose for the cameras and say pretty words about workers. But after the Democrats get elected they pretty much do the same as the Republicans. The Democrats call out the police and even the National Guard to attack picket lines, just like the Republicans.

Q. So if both the Democrats and the Republicans are against the workers then what should the working people do?

A. The working people must build their own party. The working people need a workers party. A workers party would fight to double minimum wage, a workers party would fight for free quality medical care for all Americans, a workers party would fight for the rights of all workers regardless of their race or gender or religion or their sexual preference or national origin. A workers party would seek to smash through all these barriers that divide workers against each other. A workers party would unite all workers together to support doubling our minimum wage, to support quality affordable housing for all, to support decent pensions and better social security benefits for our older people. A workers party would also take a stand against war. A workers party would also defend immigrant workers.

Q. But some people argue that immigrant workers are stealing jobs from American workers. What do you say to that?

A. The American economy has historically been one of the most dynamic economies in the world. America has always produced many jobs. However, now the employers are moving jobs overseas. The employers are moving manufacturing jobs to China. And the employers are moving professional jobs to India and other places like that. The reason that there's not enough jobs to go around is because the bosses are taking our jobs out of the country. We must understand that the politicians are using the immigrants as a scapegoat. Our country is in difficult times. The bosses have moved too many jobs abroad. We are in two wars at the same time. The economy is in horrible shape because the bankers and the fat cats on Wall Street have damaged it very badly with their greed. Instead of scapegoating immigrants we should understand that it is the politicians and rich people and the big corporations who are responsible for the fact that American workers are suffering so badly during these hard times. We should understand that the immigrants have nothing to do with our problems. The immigrants are just scapegoats. The problem is with the rich people and the politicians and big corporations who are all like pigs at the trough. It is the rich people and the politicians who are ruining our economy and destroying our nation. Not the immigrants – we've always had immigrants. American native-born and immigrant workers laboring together have made the United States of America one of the most powerful and wealthiest nations on earth. Unfortunately, the wealth does not find its way into the hands of those who actually work for a living! The vast majority of the wealth finds its way into the hands of the rich and powerful, who are often not doing the work themselves.

Q. But with their investments and their knowledge and expertise the rich people actually help to improve our economy, wouldn't you say so?

A. How much knowledge and expertise does it take to

drink champagne and eat caviar? Any idiot can do that! The rich people take and take from the country and they give back nothing. There may have been a time – like in the 19th century – when the rich people actually invested in our country. The rich people built factories, they built railroads – well, actually the workers built those things and the rich people financed the development of those projects. However, today the rich people take the money – the money that they make from the sweat of the workers – and the rich people move that money outside of the country and they put it in Switzerland and the Cayman Islands. The rich people also move our jobs abroad. The rich people do not take the money that they make from our labor and reinvest in our country anymore. So we would be better off without these rich people.

Q. So what do you propose to do with these rich people?

A. I would like to see them picking up garbage off the ground for food stamps. I would also like to see the Democrat and Republican politicians picking up garbage off the ground for food stamps as well. (Laughs) However, I have heard it said by members of a Trotskyist group that former members of the ruling class would have the right to a job at the same wages as everybody else, and that members of the former ruling class that work a job and stay out of trouble should be allowed to be productive members of society. However, after a workers revolution a workers government would have to defend itself against anyone who took up arms against the workers government or anyone who incited violence against a workers government. A workers government would also

111

have to defend itself against people who financed violent counterrevolution. Such elements would have to be crushed in order to prevent widespread bloodshed. Because in the past counterrevolutionary elements – like the Contras in Nicaragua and the white forces during the Civil War in Russia caused a lot of suffering and death and needless violence.

Q. So a workers government wouldn't necessarily line up all of its opponents against the wall and shoot them?

A. Of course not. Not unless they took up arms against a workers government, or financed or incited or advocated a violent counterrevolution. Contrary to stereotype communists do not believe in pointless violence and pointless repression. But I'm sure we could agree that after a workers government took power a workers government would have to defend itself if certain elements took up arms against the government or certain elements financed counterrevolution. After the workers revolution in Russia in 1917 it was the counterrevolutionaries who were responsible for much of the violence and bloodshed. The workers government under Lenin and Trotsky merely sought to defend itself.

Q. But many people died during communist rule in the Soviet Union – isn't that true?

A. First of all it wasn't communist rule, it was Stalinist rule. Stalin murdered, imprisoned, or exiled to Siberia most of the members of the Communist Party Central Committee that lead the revolution. It was the Stalinist bureaucracy who murdered and imprisoned many innocent people

– including many communists. It was the Stalinists who murdered Communists like Leon Trotsky. Leon Trotsky was a co-leader of the 1917 revolution along with Lenin.

Q. But haven't you heard that power corrupts absolutely? Wouldn't a workers government in America or any other part of the world go the same way as the Soviet Union?

A. Not necessarily. It all depends on the circumstances. It's important to understand what happened in the Soviet Union. It's easy to be intellectually lazy and ignorant and wave off history with a simple statement like, "power corrupts absolutely". To understand history one has to study it. The Communist Party in the Soviet Union inherited a country that was economically backward, a country that had huge amounts of illiteracy, a country that had a very small working class at that time, a country that had been devastated by World War I, a country that had been severely damaged by the violence unleashed by counterrevolutionary forces backed by countries like the USA. Another problem is that in the beginning days of the Soviet Union there weren't enough educated people to assume the positions of the bureaucracy. So the old bureaucrats under the Czar continued to be the bureaucrats under the new Soviet Union. And guess whose sons were in college becoming educated to become the next bureaucrats? The sons of the bureaucrats where the ones in college studying to become the nation's next generation of bureaucrats. Hence, the Communists were actually isolated. The bureaucrats had more and more power with each passing year. Lenin repeatedly said that in order for the Soviet Union to survive they needed a workers revolution in an advanced country like Germany so that the Soviet Union wouldn't be so isolated. However, when leftist workers attempted a revolution in Germany they were squashed by the Social Democrats. Hence, the Soviet Union stood alone. The situation made it difficult to have a full-fledged workers democracy in the Soviet Union. Instead, the bureaucracy took control and threw the communists out. The bureaucracy killed many of the communists. The country was communist in name only. The bureaucrats ran the country. It you had told Lenin that the Soviet Union would survive 70 years under such conditions Lenin would have laughed at you and told you to stop smoking so much opium! Lenin said that the Soviet Union would not survive long without a revolution in an advanced country. He was wrong. In spite of being ruled by a horrible Stalinist bureaucracy the superiority of the planned economy in the Soviet Union not only helped the Soviet Union to survive 70 years but it also helped the Soviet Union to become the second most powerful country on the earth. The superiority of the planned economy also allowed the Soviet workers to enjoy the highest standard of living that they ever enjoyed in their history! As many people know after the fall of the planned economy in the Soviet Union and the re-introduction of capitalism there the living standard of the workers has fallen tremendously.

Q. But doesn't a planned economy hurt creativity? And doesn't the capitalist economy encourage creativity?

A. Under capitalism there certainly are certain types of creativity. There are lots of people who are paid money to try and figure out the best way to sell you their brand of toilet paper. Hence, under capitalism there is lots of creativity in terms of coming up with creative ways to convince you to wipe your ass with a particular brand of toilet paper. I don't think that's the kind of creativity the human race needs.

Q. (Laughs) I mean, what I'm trying to say is that doesn't the capitalist system encourage innovation? I think the problem with a planned economy is that it's too stagnant – isn't a planned economy more stagnant and less dynamic than the capitalist one?

A. I think there's innovation in some capitalist countries. But in most capitalist countries there isn't much innovation at all. I've been to over 50 countries on this planet in Latin America, Europe, the Middle East, and Asia. In most capitalist countries you have cheap labor and because the labor is cheap there is not much incentive for innovation. Actually what I see in much of the capitalist world is a waste of labor resources. There are able-bodied men who can't find a job – lots of them! There's women staying at home because there's a lack of decent childcare. There are many people on the street in Third World capitalist countries selling the exact same things that the stores around them are selling. I've lived in a number of Third World countries and that is something you see every day in capitalist third world countries – a complete lack of efficiency and innovation.

Q. But in the capitalist first world countries there's plenty of innovation – isn't that true?

A. Sure there's lots of innovation, but what kind of innovation? Is the innovation helping mankind to progress?

The United States spends endless billions coming up with new innovative ways to kill massive numbers of people with its war machine. I fail to see how that kind of innovation is beneficial to mankind! There is very little being spent on a cure for AIDS, and that's exactly the kind of innovation that the human race desperately needs. Not enough is being spent on a cure for cancer, and that's exactly the kind of innovation that the human race needs. However, there's lots of money and resources going into new innovative ways to sell people products that perhaps they don't really need. If you need something you'll go out and buy it. You don't need someone to tell you that their brand of toilet paper is better. Your own butt will tell you that!

Q. Regarding the Third World – you cite the lack of innovation and efficiency in those countries, so don't those Third World countries deserve to be poor? Because they're inefficient and lack innovation?

A. The people who have the power and money in the Third World have less incentive to innovate or make things efficient because they have such cheap labor resources at their disposal. Besides, if you're rich in a third world country you've got it good – real good! The rich people in many Third World countries are too busy having a great time with all their money to think about innovation or efficiency! (Laughs) Anyway, it's not the fault of the working people in those countries that they're poor – they often work hard but they're paid in miserly wages. Most people in the Third World are not stupid. They just don't have opportunities. In fact, most people in the Third World are smarter than

George W. Bush, the President of the United States of America. Having lived many years off and on in the Third World and having traveled widely in the Third World I can assure you that most people who live in the Third World are smarter than the current president of the United States. (Laughs) So I don't think the problem in the Third World is a lack of intelligent people who can innovate and make things more efficient. I think the problem is that the people who rule these countries just don't care about innovation and efficiency, for the reasons I talked about. In order to improve the living standards of the vast majority of humanity living in the Third World you have to completely change the system. You've got to throw capitalism in the garbage can. Because it's capitalism that is keeping these people down. It's capitalism that stifles innovation and efficiency. It's capitalism that dooms the vast mass of humanity in the Third World to suffer so much! No, those countries don't deserve to be poor. It's capitalism that's stopping those countries from being more innovative and efficient.

Q. But the Soviet Union certainly wasn't very innovative or efficient – isn't that true?

A. They were innovative and efficient enough to be the first ones to put a satellite in outer space. They were innovative and efficient enough to become a superpower – the second most powerful country in the world! They were innovative and efficient enough to give their peoples a better standard of living than they had before or since. And back during the Soviet Union working people had free medical care, affordable housing, and the right to a job. And they had all of those things because of a planned economy! But one of the things that stifled the Soviet Union was the Stalinist bureaucracy. Trotskyists called for a political revolution to oust the Stalinist bureaucracy of the Soviet Union. A political revolution would have kept the planned economy, but would have gotten rid of the Stalinist bureaucracy, installing a workers democracy.

Q. Isn't communism incompatible with democracy?

A. No it's not. What communists want is a WORKERS democracy. Right now, we live under a rich man's democracy. Right now, workers have the right to become unemployed and end up living under a bridge. Right now, workers don't have the right to free quality medical care. Right now, workers don't have the right to quality affordable housing. Right now, the landlord has the right in most places to raise your rent is much as he'd like. So you have to move out because some yuppie has the right to take over your housing. The rich people have the right to smash your union. The system is biased in favor of the bosses. Hence, we live under a dictatorship of the rich. It is the rich people that enjoy democracy, not the workers. Under a *workers* democracy working people would have many rights; including the right to a job, including the right to a much higher minimum wage than today, including the right to decent affordable housing, the right to free quality medical care, the right to free quality child care for all working women, the right to live in a society without discrimination based on race or gender or sexual preference or national origin or religion or lack thereof. Workers will enjoy many more rights under a *workers* democracy. Workers will have the right to vote for their representatives in both the local and national levels. Also, those representatives in the local and national governments will be subject to instant recall. That is, if the workers don't like a particular politician they can vote them out right away! They won't have to wait for the next elections to get rid of some bum in office. For example, if there was somebody like George Bush and he was a complete idiot (laughs) the workers would have the right to vote them out of office at any time by simple majority. They wouldn't have to wait for the next election. That's how things would work under a workers democracy.

Q. Wouldn't a workers revolution be violent?

A. Well, if the rich people said look were sorry we've been screwing you workers over for too long so we'll give up power now and let you guys have a workers government and we won't organize counterrevolution against the workers government gee that would be nice. In other words, the communists don't want violence. After a workers revolution it will be the people who are accustomed to having great wealth and power who may want to instigate violence to try to restore the old order and their old privileges. A workers government would have to defend itself.

Q. What is the difference between socialism and communism? Is socialism like what they have in certain northern European countries and communism like what they had in the Soviet Union?

A. The Soviet Union was never communist. The Stalinist

bureaucracy found it convenient to call itself communist, but the Stalinist bureaucracy killed the communists who led the October Revolution. Capitalist countries also found it convenient to call the Soviet Union and its privileged bureaucrats Communists as well – all the more to confuse workers across the world. Of course, the politicians and the rich people of the capitalist world wanted everybody to think that the Soviet Union was communist. But that's all a lie, or a gross misrepresentation, a gross misrepresentation that was convenient for all the parties involved.

Q. Well if the Soviet Union wasn't communist then what was it?

A. (Laughs)

Q. Why are you laughing?

A. Because I was trying to think of a way to explain this in simple English. However, that's not easy to do. The Soviet Union was a degenerated workers state.

Q. (Laughs) What? A degenerated workers state? What's that?

A. The Soviet Union began as a workers state. The workers came to power in the revolution of 1917. However, the situation degenerated when the Stalinist bureaucracy began to take power away from the communists. This was possible because of the circumstances I discussed earlier. The situation in the Soviet Union made it difficult to establish a workers democracy there. Remember I talked about how before the workers revolution Russia was already poor and there was lots of illiteracy at that time and the country had been devastated by World War I, and the fact that the damn bureaucrats in the early Soviet Union were the same bureaucrats who'd been the bureaucrats under the czar – so the situation degenerated for all these reasons and that's why it's a degenerated workers state. It started out as a workers state but it degenerated and the communists lost control to the Stalinist bureaucracy – so it was a degenerated workers state. It was not communism. It wasn't even socialism.

Q. Socialism – is that what they had in northern Europe? With the safety net and all that?

A. No, they did not have socialism in northern Europe. What they had in many Western European countries was capitalism with a safety net. The reason they had capitalism with a safety net is that the workers were more militant in Western Europe than in the USA. The workers in Europe fought harder for more social benefits. The workers had political parties that were more to the left of our Republicans and Democrats. That is one of the reasons that the workers had a bigger safety net, that is that they have more social programs, they had things like free medical care, free college education, better social benefits if one became unemployed or couldn't find work. So the workers had this safety net partly as a result of having more militant parties to the left of our Democrats and Republicans. Another reason that some of these capitalist Western European countries have a larger safety net than the United States is because of the proximity of so-called Communist Eastern Europe. The ruling class of the Western European capitalist countries didn't want the workers to become sympathetic to quote unquote communism. They bought off their workers with the safety net that we've been talking about. However, now that the Stalinist countries have fallen and so-called communism is no more these capitalist countries in Western Europe are trying to get rid of that safety net. They don't feel threatened by so-called communism anymore. So the safety net in those Western European countries is being taken away from the workers. Hence, those Western European countries were never socialist. They are capitalist with a safety net. No nation has even reached the stage of socialism.

Q. So you believe that no nation has even reached the stage of socialism? Perhaps that's because socialism and communism are nice ideas in theory, but they cannot work in practice?

A. Of course socialism can work in practice. The Soviet Union rose from being a poverty-stricken backward nation into becoming the second most powerful country in the world – thanks to a planned economy. That proves a planned economy is superior to a capitalist one. Look at all the economic misery in the capitalist world today! Having a planned economy helped to industrialize the Soviet Union and give the working people of the Soviet Union a better standard of living than they have in capitalist Russia today. However, even though they had a planned economy the Soviet Union never reach socialism. As I explained before the Soviet Union was a degenerated workers state.

It never had workers democracy. It did not have socialism. You cannot have socialism in just one country. A workers revolution would have to spread to many countries – particularly economically advanced countries in the first world in order for the human race to achieve socialism. Under socialism everyone would have the right to a job, everyone would have a decent standard of living, people would be paid according to their work, everyone who works would receive free quality medical care and free quality child care, affordable decent housing would be human right, etc. Look at how the rich people and the politicians have run our country into the ground, gotten us into two wars at the same time, and put millions of Americans behind prison bars – most of it because of drugs, not to mention that in many places of our nation the school system is in shambles, as is public transportation, and the medical system stinks. That's how the rich people run our nation. It's time for the working people to rule. The working people must rule not just America but everywhere across the world.

Q. Okay. You just described socialism. So then what's communism? And what's the difference between socialism and communism?

A. Yes I just described socialism and how it would work. Socialism would be a workers democracy where workers would elect their local and national representatives, and workers would also have the power to kick any politician out any time by simple majority recall vote. Workers would have all the rights I talked about earlier. Communism is a much later stage of economic development that comes after socialism. Communism would not be achieved for a long time. Simply the world is not economically developed enough for communism. Under communism the people would have all the same rights that they have under socialism, but the economy will be much more advanced. There's no greed leap forward to communism. It may not even happen in our lifetimes. I cannot even invision communism. It is way too far in the future. But, I can see that socialism in our lifetimes is a very real possibility. A society where everyone has the right to work, where everyone has the right to a decent education, where everyone has the right to free quality child care for their children and free quality medical care for everyone, and workers have the right to elect their own leaders and recall them by popular vote at any time. Socialism is the next stage of human development. If we do not reach socialism then certainly the capitalist powers of the world will eventually unleash a nuclear war and the human race will become extinct. Therefore, the choice is clear. The choice is capitalism and barbarism or socialism and a decent life for every human being on the planet.

Q. If someone wanted to find out more about socialism and communism what would you suggest they do?

A. I would suggest they read. I would read the following books: *Ten Days That Shook the World* by John Reed, *Last Will and Testament* by Lenin, *Socialism: Utopian and Scientific* by Frederick Engels, *Wage Labor and Capital* by Karl Marx , *State and Revolution* by Lenin, *Imperialism: The Final Stage of Capitalism* by Lenin, *What Is to Be Done?* by Lenin, *Left-Wing Communism: an Infantile Disorder* by Lenin, and *Permanent Revolution* by Trotsky. Read the newspapers of all the groups claiming to be socialist and communist, and find out which one is truly revolutionary. You will find that the vast majority of them are reformist.

Q. Are you a member of any political group?

A. No. At this time I'm not a member of any political group. I speak for no one but myself and the interests of working people and poor people across the world.

The Latest Economic Crisis

An Interview with Wolf Larsen

Question: So Wolf, what do you think of this latest economic crisis? Answer: Man, what a mess! I guess the bankers and the fat cats on Wall Street really screwed up the economy this time! But capitalism has always had its ups and downs. That's just the way it is.

Q. That's just the way it is? What about all the people losing their jobs? It's one of the highest unemployment rates since the Great Depression!

A. I know. That's the nature of capitalism. Lots of human suffering. You notice that the first thing that the politicians in Washington did was bail out all the fat cats in the banking industry and on Wall Street. And yet they haven't gotten around to bailing out homeowners who are being thrown out on the street. The fact is the politicians both Democrat and Republican don't care about all the human suffering that's going to be caused by this crisis. What the politicians of both parties care about is saving the asses of the rich.

Q. What caused this economic crisis?

A. Too much speculation. Too much paper wealth. The

ruling class used to invest in our country. They invested in factories, they invested in railroads, they invested in all forms of infrastructure. But now the rich people of our country don't want to invest in our country anymore. Now instead of investing in factories the rich people prefer to come up with predatory schemes to enrich themselves at the expense of the working people.

Q. Where do you think the economy is headed?

A. Down. The economy has been going down for the past 30 years. Not just in the past year. When I was a child back in the 1970s I lived in a very prosperous and powerful nation. Our nation is still relatively prosperous – at least compared to Third World countries – but America is nowhere near as prosperous as it used to be. That's because the rich people have closed a lot of our factories. We've lost much of our industrial base. And when a country loses its industrial base it loses its very foundation. Now the rich people are outsourcing the professional jobs to places like India. So not only have we lost much of our industrial base, but now we're losing a big chunk of the information economy as well. A lot of professional jobs are going overseas, just like the blue collar jobs before. Of course, the workers in China and India and across the world are not our enemies, they are workers like ourselves. All workers across the world are our brothers and sisters. It is the rich people and their big corporations that are the enemies of working people.

Q. So too much speculation and bad lending practices and

the loss of the industrial sector is what caused this latest economic crisis in your opinion?

A. Bad lending practices is an understatement. The lending practices were downright predatorial. All the fat cats who were giving out predatorial loans didn't care if these people lost their homes in the future. All that the predatorial lenders cared about was making lots of money real fast. But that's the nature of capitalism. The rich people get richer and working people get screwed. Losing our industrial base is the single biggest reason that our economy is falling. You can't have a powerful wealthy nation without a strong industrial base to support it. Instead of creating more wealth with industry and with a higher standard of living all the economy was doing was creating paper wealth – or speculation – and that is not a healthy economy. Capitalism is not a healthy type of economy.

Q. Is the problem really the entire system of capitalism? Isn't the problem a lack of regulation governing the economic system? Wouldn't better regulation have stopped this crisis?

A . Up-and-down cycles are the very nature of capitalism. It's a crazy irrational economic system. There will always be economic crashes under capitalism. Under capitalism in the best of times there's lots of human suffering. In the worst of times there's even more human suffering. The rich people just keep getting richer. That's the nature of capitalism. Regulation may or may not prevent the worst abuses, but no amount of regulation is going to stop the fact that capitalism is an up-and-down craziness of boom and bust. Capitalism is irrational. And no amount of regulation will change that.

Q. So you don't support more regulation in the financial sector in order to prevent a future crisis like the one that just happened?

A. Instead of trying to regulate the system lets just throw capitalism in the garbage can.

Q. But the new President of the United States seems to be a very talented individual. And he has excellent advisers around him. Don't you think perhaps he could save the economy?

A. No. Mr. Obama might be more intelligent than George Bush, but that will not save endless millions of people from being unemployed because of an economic crisis. Capitalism is always having economic crisis. It is a boom and bust system. Capitalism was going boom and bust long before Obama or any of us were born. Regardless of whatever new regulations they may impose capitalism will continue to have periods of crisis in the future because that is the nature of capitalism. The only solution is to get rid of capitalism, and replace it with socialism. Under a planned economy there will be no more boom and bust. Under socialism everyone will have the right to a job. Whether you build a bus or drive a train or provide medical services – everyone will do something. There will be no more capitalists. There would be no more speculation. All the capitalist predators will have their ill begotten wealth confiscated, and they will have to get real jobs. They won't be able to screw up our economy anymore. And the politicians will have to get real jobs too. I can already see Obama, George Bush and Dick Cheney, Bill and Hillary Clinton all working at McDonald's together. But I don't think we'll trust George Bush in the kitchen – everyone might get food poisoning that guy is so incompetent. I think with Dick Cheney we'll just let him clean the bathroom and wash the floors. Mr. Obama has good people skills – so he can work the cash register and smile at everyone at the front. Bill and Hillary can do all the hamburger flipping. And that George Bush will make an excellent clown, we'll dress him up like Ronald McDonald and he can greet all the customers as they come in, and entertain the children. (Laughs)

Who Are the Real Terrorists?

An Interview with Wolf Larsen

Question: So what do you think should be done about terrorism?

Answer: Well, this depends on how you define terrorism and who the real terrorists are. I would argue that if a police officer shoots an innocent black man to death that that is terrorism. I would argue that if the American war machine drops a bomb on a family having dinner in Afghanistan or Pakistan that that is terrorism. I would argue that what the American government did to the people of Vietnam was large-scale terrorism. I would argue that what the Israeli military is doing to the Palestinian people is terrorism. And I certainly condemn terrorism.

Q. But what about the terrorists who strap a bomb to their body and then explode their bomb and kill themselves and innocent civilians and soldiers?

A. I condemn the killing of innocent civilians. As far as I'm concerned terrorism is defined by the killing of innocent civilians. If someone straps a bomb to his body and kills innocent civilians than that person is a despicable terrorist.

131

Wolf Larsen

If the President of the United States of America orders bombs to be dropped on a foreign country than the American President is a terrorist. Terrorists are despicable. Someone who kills foreign soldiers occupying his country is not a terrorist however. There is a difference between killing innocent civilians and killing foreign soldiers that are occupying your country. Remember, during the American Revolutionary war we fought the Redcoats. The Redcoats were a foreign army on our soil. When we killed the Redcoats we were not terrorists, because we were shooting at foreign soldiers on our soil. Therefore, persons in whatever country that kill foreign soldiers occupying their land are not terrorists. Terrorists are people that kill innocent civilians. The United States government kills more innocent civilians in its various wars than any other terrorist on the planet. Therefore, the United States government is the biggest terrorist on the planet.

Q. You call the American government the biggest terrorist on the planet. But the American government says that it is involved in a war against terrorism. That's kind of ironic.

A. Yes it is. It's very ironic that the biggest terrorist in the world – which is the American government – says that it is in a war against terrorism. The United States is not in a war against terrorism. The United States says that it is in a war against terrorism, but that is a lie. The United States uses rhetoric about terrorism as a pretext to go to war in Iraq because Iraq has huge oil reserves. The US government was interested in Iraq's oil reserves, the war in Iraq had nothing to do with terrorism. The United States government said it went to war in Afghanistan to fight terrorism, but ironically the biggest terrorist in Afghanistan is the United States government. The United States war machine has killed countless innocent civilians in Afghanistan, as well as in neighboring Pakistan.

Q. But didn't the United States government have to fight in Afghanistan to punish the terrorists for the 9/11 attacks?

A. There appear to be many unanswered questions about the 9/11 attacks, and there are many who believe that 9/11 was an inside job. But regardless of whether 9/11 was an inside job or not I think it's obvious that the US government looks for various excuses to make all these constant wars all the time. The US government used the whole 9/11 incident as an excuse to go to war. It's tragic that all those people died in 9/11. It's also tragic that so many have died in the wars in Afghanistan and Pakistan. It is also a disgusting shame that the politicians of both parties used 9/11 to eliminate many of our civil liberties with a vile piece of legislation called the Patriot Act.

Q. But wasn't the Patriot Act necessary to protect the American people from terrorism?

A. And who's going to protect us from the biggest terrorist in the world – which is the United States government. The cops shooting innocent black men to death in the streets – now that's terrorism. And the same police that are shooting innocent black men are the same police that are breaking the strikes of working-class people and escorting the scabs into the workplaces to take their jobs. These same police protect the interests of the landlords and the banks and help to evict people who fall behind on their mortgages and rent. Evicting people out in the streets and into the cold – now that's a form of terrorism. Think of the terror of a middle-aged person who has lost her job and can't find another and is worried that she will never be employed again. Don't you think that person is terrified? And what of the terror of the dozen black activists and their children of the MOVE organization in Philadelphia in may 1985 when they were murdered by the police on orders of Wilson Goode – what about their terror? What about the terror of the people who lived in Waco Texas who were murdered by the police forces gathered around their compound? What about their terror? Terrorism is wrong! And the biggest terrorist in the world can be found in Washington, DC. Terrorists wear police uniforms here in America. Here in America the CEOs of large corporations are engaged in a kind of economic terrorism against working-class Americans – eliminating jobs and throwing Americans out of their homes. So we have to be clear who the worst terrorists are. And yes I certainly condemn terrorism.

What Is the State and What Is Its Nature?

An Interview with Wolf Larsen

Question: What do Marxists mean by the state?

Answer: What we mean by the state is not like the state of Indiana in the United States or the state of Amazonas in Brazil. Basically, the state is the entire government from the President all the way down to the police officer. The state includes the army, the police, the courts, the prisons – all of that is the apparatus of the state. I am not a great theoretician, but I can tell you for sure that most states on our planet today are dominated by the wealthy. These states dominated by the wealthy preside over capitalist economies that benefit only a privileged few. These states use their police forces, their armies, their courts, and bureaucracies to foster the domination of the rich over the working people.

Q. But if these states are Democratic then can't the working people use democracy to change the nature of the state?

A. Let me make something absolutely clear. All the democracies currently on this planet are democracies dominated by the rich people. In addition, most of the dictatorships on this planet rule in the interests of the rich people as well. It is obviously better to live in a democracy dominated by the rich than to live in a dictatorship dominated by their rich. In a dictatorship you rarely have freedom of speech. In a democracy there is more freedom of speech – up to a point.

Q. So are you saying that even in a democracy the workers don't have much freedom?

A. In a capitalist democracy the workers have more freedom than in a capitalist dictatorship. That is obvious. However, in a capitalist democracy the workers still do not have the right to a job, they do not have the right to a decent minimum wage, they don't have the right to quality affordable housing, etc. In order to have these kinds of rights you have to have a major change. You have to end the democracy of the rich and replace it with a democracy of the working class. The democracy of the working class is socialism. In a democracy of the rich the government often oppresses the workers in a manner similar to a dictatorship. When the bourgeoisie feel threatened by the workers – such as if the workers have a general strike that shuts down everything – regardless of whether the state is a bourgeois democracy or a bourgeois dictatorship – the apparatus of the state with its police and army and courts and jails often comes down very hard on the workers and attacks the workers and imprisons the workers and workers are often beat up by the police. Sometimes the police shoot down the workers in cold blood. So you see the state is an instrument of oppression where one class dominates the other class. The rich use the police, the army, the courts, the laws, and the prisons to keep the workers down. The police and army are the apparatus of the state – it is how the rich enforce their rule upon the workers.

Q. I don't believe you answered my question. Can't the workers use democracy to reform the state?

A. I believe I have answered your question. It is impossible to change the nature of the state. The state is an instrument of class oppression. The rich people use the state to oppress the workers. It is not possible to change the nature of the state. When workers elect supposedly pro-worker politicians to office those politicians almost always betray the interests of the workers. What workers can do is engage in social struggle that wins them some rights. For example, during the period of the Great Depression there was a great deal of social struggle by workers and the unemployed. In order to help ensure its survival the bourgeoisie gave in to some of these demands and the government implemented things like unemployment insurance, Social Security, and things like that. These were things that the workers and the unemployed fought for. During the 1960s you see some similarities to what happened in the 1930s. The black people of our nation made social struggle for racial equality. Because of this social struggle the government enacted civil rights legislation. None of these reforms however changes the nature of the state. The state is an instrument of class oppression where the rich use the state to oppress the workers. In order to calm all the social struggle down the rich sometimes give in on some points and enact legislation like unemployment insurance, Social Security, and civil rights laws. But inevitably the bourgeoisie seeks to backtrack. The bourgeoisie seeks to eliminate the gains that working-class and minorities made in social struggle. That's why you see the government later weakening social programs and civil rights laws in periods of lesser social struggle.

Q. So it sounds like under capitalism there's constant struggle between the rich and the working people.

A. That's right. The rich want to pay their workers as little as possible. The workers want more money. The rich want to cut back on or eliminate as many social programs as possible. In periods of less social struggle that's exactly what the rich people's government does – it cuts back on social programs. In times of more social struggle the bourgeoisie often give a little – and their government introduces more social programs or increases funding for social programs. The government does not increase social programs or create civil rights legislation because they have bleeding hearts and are concerned about the workers, the politicians do this in order to avert social struggle. It's like when there are more strikes and protests the rich people's government gives in a little in order to cool things off but as soon as things cool off then the rich man's government seeks to backtrack and undermine the civil rights legislation, they seek to lower funding for Social Security, and things like that.

Q. If social struggle brings more benefits to workers and minorities and women then all the workers and minorities and women need to do is engage in constant social struggle – isn't that true?

A. Social struggle can be good. It can help the workers and minorities and women and gays achieve many rights and other things. However, social struggle is dangerous. The police beat people up. The police shoot people. And if that's not enough the rich man's government calls in the army or the National Guard and they start shooting people. Social struggle can turn into a bloody mess! Social struggle without revolution does not permanently solve the problem of capitalism and the many problems that capitalism brings about – things like war, poverty, unemployment, racial discrimination, homophobia, gender discrimination, and so on and so forth. Social struggle is better than nothing, but it doesn't permanently resolve the problem of the state.

Q. So how do you solve the problem of the state?

A. You have to change the nature of the state. Currently the nature of the state is that it is a bourgeois state. It is a state dominated by the rich people. So you have to throw the bourgeois state in the garbage and replace it with a workers state.

Q. So how do you do that? Do you vote Democrat? Aren't the Democrats more for the workers?

A. (Laughs) What the Democrats and the Republicans represent are two different wings of the ruling class. The ruling class are the rich people. You have to throw the Democrats and the Republicans in the garbage can, because they are rich peoples parties. The same is true of the Labour Party in England. The Labour Party in England has become a rich peoples party. It says a bunch of pretty words about workers and has the title "labor" but basically all the Labor Party cares about is helping the rich. What reformist parties like Labor and the Democrats seek to do is to confuse the workers and spawn illusions in the rich people's government. That is, they want to fool the working people and the poor people into believing that they can reform the government in the working man's favor. But after these reformist parties like Labor and the Democrats get elected they pretty much do the same as the Republicans or the Tories. Within the framework of a bourgeois democracy different wings of the ruling class can argue out loud about their differences of opinion. With their different political parties and newspapers and television news outlets the different wings of the ruling class argue with each other about this, that, and the other thing. In a capitalist dictatorship, on the other hand, it's much more difficult for the different sections of the ruling class to discuss out in the open their differences. What's more, in a capitalist dictatorship some asshole decides what's best for the rich. So often the ruling class prefers a bourgeois democracy over a bourgeois dictatorship, because the bourgeoisie have more freedom of speech to discuss and argue amongst themselves. In addition, in a bourgeois democracy the workers often have more illusions that they can reform the system. And thus in that manner it is easier for the rich to dupe the workers into submission, or at least in tolerating the capitalist system. Sometimes the bourgeoisie resorts to a dictatorship because they're simply just too afraid of the workers to have democracy. And then there's fascism.

Q. What about fascism?

A. There are different aspects of fascism. There are the Ku Klux Klan and the neo-Nazis in our country who seek to divide white workers against black workers, immigrants, gays, etc. This aspect of fascism helps to weaken the working class by dividing one section of the workers against the other. Another aspect of fascism is the fascist state. The fascist state – like in the case of Nazi Germany – rules on behalf of the interests of the rich and the big corporations. The fascist state under Hitler smashed the unions and all the other workers organizations. One of the reasons that the bourgeoisie in Germany resorted to supporting Hitler and the Nazis is that they wanted to crush the workers organizations, which they felt had become too powerful. In addition, the bourgeoisie decided that the Weimer Republic government (which was a democracy) was simply too weak to enforce its rule. The Weimer Republic government was ruling on behalf of the rich people in Germany, but the Weimer Republic government was ineffective. And that is one of the reasons why the German bourgeoisie turned to fascism and helped Hitler and his Nazi party come to power.

Q. What about anarchy?

A. Anarchists want to do away with the state entirely. How are the workers going to defend themselves against violent fascists and everything else that the bourgeoisie throws their way if the workers do not have a state of their own to defend themselves with? Anarchy is just plain naïveté. It can never work. If the workers do not have their own state than they will be ruthlessly crushed. The workers must have their own state so that they can defend themselves.

Q. So how can workers get a state of their own? A state that will rule in the workers interests?

A. A bourgeois state – whether it's a democracy or dictatorship or fascist – will never rule in the interests of the workers. A bourgeois state might give some social programs to appease the workers at times of social struggle, but a bourgeois state will always remain a bourgeois state. It may change its form – it may go from being a democracy to dictatorship or may go to fascism or even a monarchy – but a bourgeois state regardless of its form continues to rule in the interests of the rich. Therefore, the workers have to SMASH the bourgeois state and replace it with a workers state.

Q. How do you replace a bourgeois state with a workers state?

A. First the working class needs political independence from the bourgeoisie. The workers have to divorce themselves from reformist parties like the Democrats and the fake "Labor" party in Britain. The workers need their own party. The workers need a workers party. A workers party will fight for the working class. The workers party will engage in struggles like supporting strikes, supporting gay rights, supporting women's rights, supporting minority rights, etc. The workers party also seeks to raise the political consciousness of the workers, and help them to understand that ultimately they have to replace the bourgeois state with a workers state.

Q. And how do you replace the bourgeois state with a workers state? With a revolution?

A. Yes. Exactly.

Q. But wouldn't a revolution be violent?

A. Socialists do not seek violence. However, it is very likely that a workers state – which can also be called a socialist government – would have to defend itself against the bourgeoisie. Over and over again in the past whenever working people rose up to take what was rightfully theirs the bourgeoisie responded with violence. Therefore, a workers government would have to defend itself. A workers government would have its own army and possibly its own police force to defend itself. Or instead of a police force a workers government might create integrated workers guards that would patrol the cities and the countryside. These integrated workers guards would be allied with a workers government. The integrated workers guards might work with the police or they might entirely replace the police. The state has been called "armed bodies of men". That is what the state is – armed bodies of men and women. In the case of a bourgeois state the army and the police oppress the workers in the interests of the rich. In the case of a workers state the army, police, and integrated workers guards oppress the rich and defend the interests of the workers.

Q. So under socialism – which is a workers state – the army and the police remain unchanged?

A. Not exactly. The police force would have to be completely changed. The entire police force would have to be fired and replaced. You would need new police officers who would be interested in defending a workers state. The new police officers would keep the peace, arrest thieves and violent individuals. But the main function of the police in a workers state would be to defend the workers state. Under capitalism the main function of the police is to defend the interests of the bourgeoisie. Hence, the old police force would have to be replaced with new police officers who are sympathetic to a workers government. The army on the other hand might be different. I think it would be necessary to replace the generals and any officers suspected of being sympathetic to the bourgeoisie. In addition, measures would have to be taken to make sure that generals and higher officers of the old capitalist army do not become generals and higher officers in a counterrevolutionary army. But rank-and-file soldiers and lower officers who are sympathetic to a workers government could remain in the armed forces of the workers state. On the other hand those soldiers and officers who were not sympathetic to a workers state would have to be dismissed. I would argue that any discharged soldiers and police officers should be offered new jobs. You want elements like that to have a decent income so that they'll have more incentive to stay out of trouble.

On how the army could be organized after the workers revolution one should consult Leon Trotsky's writings on the subject, as Trotsky was the leader of the Red Army when it squashed the counterrevolution. In the case of the police officers of the old capitalist regime it would be important for a workers government to watch them carefully, to make sure that they stay out of trouble. It is important to realize that immediately following the change from a bourgeois government to a workers government there will be many potentially counterrevolutionary elements which may want to overthrow a workers government. A workers government would have to defend itself against this.

Q. It sounds somewhat repressive.

A. Remember that a state is an instrument of class oppression. If it is a bourgeois state than the bourgeoisie oppress the workers. If it is a workers state then the workers oppress the bourgeoisie. The bourgeoisie need workers because after all somebody has to do the work. Somebody has to provide services. Somebody needs to build things. However, under socialism the workers will have no need for the bourgeoisie. When I say the bourgeoisie I do not mean well-paid specialists. Brain surgeons, rocket scientists, and others with important skills will have a very nice standard of living under socialism. However, under socialism there will be no need for people who sit around eating caviar and drinking champagne and not working and living off of some gigantic inheritance. There will be no need for people like that. All of the money of the billionaires and multimillionaires will be confiscated and used for the public good. Under socialism everyone has to work. I imagine that those who enjoyed a caviar and champagne lifestyle under capitalism are going to be very upset when they find out that they have to get out of bed in the morning and go to work or else they don't eat. A workers government would have to take appropriate measures and ruthlessly crush any attempt of counterrevolution by the former bourgeoisie and anyone who would aid them. A workers government would have to defend itself against any counterrevolutionary elements. As the former elements of the bourgeoisie and their henchmen and sympathizers die off of old age and it becomes clear that there is no longer a counterrevolutionary danger then slowly the state will need fewer police officers and fewer soldiers. In addition, a socialist government would have to maintain a strong military to defend itself from capitalist countries. But over time as capitalism fades from the earth and the remaining elements of the former bourgeoisie and their sympathizers and henchmen die from old age and the threats to the workers state diminish then the state as an oppressive instrument will gradually fade away. But during this whole time the workers themselves will have lots of democracy. It will be the workers who enjoy democracy. Workers will not be repressed. Only counterrevolutionary elements will be repressed, because the workers state must defend itself against any danger, in order to keep the peace.

Watch out for Reformist Parties and Reformist Movements

An Interview with Wolf Larsen

Question: What's wrong with reformist parties and reformist movements? Isn't it good to reform the system?

Answer: It's important not to have illusions in reformist parties or reformist movements. It's possible that in times of social struggle a bourgeois government might give the workers and the poor some social programs, which some might call "reform". At other times a bourgeois government might curb some of the worst excesses of the capitalist system, but that doesn't change the fact that the bourgeoisie are still in power. They might even throw out one capitalist politician or political party or dictator and replace them with another capitalist politician or political party or dictator. But the bourgeoisie still remain in power. As socialists we welcome any changes which are beneficial to workers and the poor, but at the same time we point out that it's important that workers and the poor not have illusions in a bourgeois government. Sometimes when workers have too many illusions in a bourgeois government this can have fatal consequences for the workers and leftists.

Q. Fatal consequences? What fatal consequences?

A. Look at what happened in Chile in 1973. The workers and students and leftists together elected Allende into the government. The government was supposedly a "socialist" or pro-worker government. Anyway these "socialists" or "leftists" or "progressive forces" in the government did not smash the bourgeoisie and its state. The military generals remained in place. The bourgeoisie kept their economic power. When the generals and officers of the armed forces and the bourgeoisie became uncomfortable with some of the reforms of the new government they responded with a coup d'état under the leadership of General Pinochet. Many many leftist workers and students were killed. The country languished for years under the dictatorship of General Pinochet. This is what happens when the workers have illusions in the capitalist system. They pay for these illusions with their lives. It's impossible for the workers to rule a nation unless they smash the bourgeoisie and the state with which they rule. For the workers to rule the workers must destroy the bourgeoisie as a class, so that the bourgeoisie can't organize counterrevolution and later have the workers killed or jailed or whatever. The workers have to smash the bourgeois state and replace it with a workers state. The state is armed bodies of men. So the workers have to control the state, that is they have to control the armed forces and control the police apparatus. This would involve replacing the officers and generals with new officers and generals who are pro-worker, who are sympathetic to a workers state. This would also mean dismissing all of the old police officers and replacing them with new police officers who are sympathetic to a workers state, or replacing the police with armed workers guards, who would defend the interests of a workers state. If all the guns are in the hands of the henchmen of the bourgeoisie than the workers can be squashed at any time. All of the guns must be in the hands of the workers, and the workers state, so that the workers and the workers state can defend themselves against the counterrevolutionary bourgeoisie and their sympathizers and henchmen.

Q. But wasn't Allende a socialist? Didn't he call himself a socialist?

A. President Allende may have called himself a socialist, but he was no socialist. There's all kinds of tendencies that call themselves socialist or communist, but they are neither.

Q. That's kind of confusing.

A. Yes it is. And countless workers have paid with their lives for this confusion. There are political parties and individuals who call themselves socialist and communist but yet these so-called "socialists" and "communists" foster illusions that bourgeois governments can be reformed in the interests of workers. Allende thought that he could reform the Chilean government and economy to be more in favor of the workers. He was wrong. The bourgeoisie in Chile and its armed forces were not interested in being ruled by a government that was sympathetic to the workers. So the bourgeoisie and its henchmen in the police and armed forces killed Allende and many leftist workers and students as well. That's why it's important not to have illusions in the bourgeoisie. You can pay for these illusions with your life. The historical examples of this happening over and over again are endless. Back *before* Mao the Communist Party of China worked closely with a general named Chiang Kai-shek. Chiang Kai-shek wanted to kick out the Japanese invaders out of China. Chiang Kai-shek was also interested in reforming the Chinese system. So the communists thought that he was a "progressive" ally. But the workers have no progressive allies in the bourgeoisie and in the bourgeoisie's henchmen in the police and armed forces. The only allies the workers have in the armed forces are potentially the rank-and-file soldiers and lower officers. Anyway, when Chiang Kai-shek felt that the leftist workers were becoming too influential he butchered 10,000 of them on the streets of Shanghai. 10,000 workers in Shanghai paid with their lives for their illusions that there was some "progressive" elements amongst the bourgeoisie and their henchmen in the military. Other examples include the Spanish Civil War. In the Spanish Civil War the Stalinist "Communist Party" was always telling the workers to ally themselves with some so-called "progressive" wing of the Spanish bourgeoisie. However, there is no such thing as a progressive wing of the bourgeoisie. This is an illusion. Of course the bourgeoisie might have differences amongst themselves, but when faced with a workers rebellion the bourgeoisie will always close ranks and unite and seek to crush the workers revolt, with blood if necessary. And that is exactly what happened in the Spanish Civil War. The entire Spanish bourgeoisie aligned themselves with General Franco and General Franco unleashed endless violence and killed endless numbers of leftist workers and students and anybody else he didn't like. The bourgeoisie and their henchmen want to maintain power for themselves. That is why they will always crush the workers when they feel threatened by the working class.

Q. So what you're saying, in short, is that some groups that call themselves socialist and communist are not really socialist and communist, because they perpetrate illusions in some progressive wing of the bourgeoisie. They perpetrate the illusion that the workers can change a government from bourgeoisie to proletarian through elections.

A. Precisely. A real socialist or communist group will tell the workers the truth: that in order to have a proletarian government you need to smash the bourgeoisie government and that the workers need to arm themselves to defend themselves and that a proletarian government would have to take control of the military and the police apparatus. A state is a body of armed men. Whoever controls the body of armed men is the state, and thus with brute force they decide the destiny of that nation. Currently, in the United States, behind the façade of bourgeois democracy are the armed bodies of men who make up the state. These bodies of men are the police, the National Guard, and the army. While it is possible that rank-and-file soldiers in the National Guard and the army will one day rebel against the bourgeois state they will only do so if they think that the workers have a chance of winning. The soldiers may be sympathetic to the workers, but in a situation of class conflict if the soldiers think that a bourgeois government will win the conflict than the soldiers will side with the bourgeoisie. This is the nature of human perseverance. However if the soldiers see that the workers have a good chance of obtaining state power and in addition the soldiers are not happy with their lot (i.e. perhaps they're sick and tired of all these wars) in that type of scenario it is possible soldiers may take the side of the workers. In this situation you have the armed soldiers and hopefully the workers are armed as well and the workers and soldiers are united in smashing the bourgeois state and replacing it with a workers state. In a workers revolution all of the politicians in the bourgeoisie state are thrown in the garbage, as are all of the highest functionaries. The workers then elect new representatives straight from the factory and office floor. Obviously, the white-collar workers and the blue-collar workers must be united. Only the workers will vote. The supervisors will not have any power. All high-level supervisors and functionaries will be replaced with new ones who are sympathetic to a workers government.

Q. But aren't there countries that have socialist or communist parties in their governments and yet the bourgeoisie does not make violence against the workers and the socialist or communist parties?

A. Yes this has happened, and is happening at this moment as well. There are political parties that call themselves "socialist" and "communist" but in reality they are very far removed from these labels. The bourgeoisie does not feel threatened by these reformist parties and movements because they are "socialist" or "communist" in name only. And that is why the reason the bourgeoisie does not respond to these types of parties being in power with violent repression. At times, due to the pressures from social struggle and other problems the bourgeoisie allow ostensibly pro-worker or "socialist" or "communist" parties to remain in power until things cool off. But when things have cooled off enough they push those political parties out of power – sometimes peacefully and sometimes violently. At other times the bourgeoisie allow those parties to remain in power as long as it's pro-worker or socialist or communist in name only. There are many so-called pro-worker or "socialist" or "communist" parties that actually indeed represent the interests of the bourgeoisie. I even heard of a so-called "communist" politician in local office in Brazil who voted against an increase in the minimum wage! These politicians may belong to so-called "socialist" or "communist" parties but they are really governing in the interests of the bourgeoisie. The bourgeoisie may give in a little during times of social struggle – that is, they may give the workers unemployment compensation or free medical care or civil rights legislation – but that does not change the fact that the government remains a bourgeois government. The workers need a workers government. However, in order to install a workers government it has to be the right moment. In October 1917 it was the right moment for a workers revolution in Russia. The workers were fed up with their wages and other things. The soldiers were fed up with the war. And the majority of peasants were fed up too. And luckily in October 1917 there was a political party in Russia – the Bolshevik party – that was ready to lead the workers, soldiers, and peasants into a proletarian revolution.

Q. Throughout history some people have argued that in some countries the revolution must occur in two stages. That is, first there must be the first revolution to make democracy or independence, depending on the circumstances of that country. The second stage of the revolution is the workers revolution. What do you think of that?

A. Well, for some people there's not much difference between the mouth in their face and the anus that's down below – because nothing but a bunch of shit comes out. Anyway, the argument favoring a two-stage revolution is a bunch of old archaic nonsense. Let me explain something elementary. This is Marxism 101. There's two sides – there's the bourgeoisie on one side and there's workers on the other – and you're on one side or you're on the other. You either have a bourgeois government, or you have a workers government. The 10,000 Chinese workers who tragically lost their lives to the General Chiang Kai-shek believed in that two-stage revolution nonsense – and looked what happened to them. In the Spanish Civil War the so-called "Communist" party there had pushed that line about the two-stage revolution there as well – and their allusions were shot down by General Franco's bullets. To see how a workers revolution works look no further than the October Revolution in Russia in 1917. That's the way it's done. The October Revolution in 1917 brought the working class to power. That's the way you do it. You bring *workers* democracy and workers to power all in one swift action – and that action is a workers revolution. For more reading on the subject I suggest you try Leon Trotsky's *Permanent Revolution*.

Q. Do you think a workers revolution would look the same in the first world and the third world?

A. Absolutely. In both the first and third worlds it's the same problem: the workers have to have a revolution to dislodge the bourgeoisie from power. The workers have to seize state power. Workers have to control the armed bodies of men that make up the state. It's the same in every part of the world, in both first and third world countries. Some people say that in some Third World countries there is an "anti-imperialist" wing of the bourgeoisie that will stand up to the big bad imperialist powers like the United States. They say that workers should unite with this "anti-imperialist" wing of the bourgeoisie in Third World countries. This is utter nonsense. If the bourgeoisie in first or third world countries feel threatened by the workers then the bourgeoisie will smash the workers using the armed bodies of men that make up the state, and the workers will pay for their illusions with their blood and lives. Sometimes some Third World ruler will stand up a little bit to some first world country like the United States. The ruler will speak a bunch of tough-sounding rhetoric. But usually all this is is a bunch of rhetoric. Sometimes his rhetoric is to help blind the working people in his country to their own grinding poverty. A ruler who temporarily stands up to some imperialist power but who later feels threatened by the working people of his own nation will crush the workers with bullets. Anyway, more often than not you will find that the bourgeoisie in Third World countries cooperate with the bourgeoisie in the first world countries. It's all about money. All these rich people care about is money. In the first world countries workers should always stand against imperialism. Every worker in a first world country like the United States should understand that his main enemy is the bourgeoisie at home, as well as the politicians and henchmen who almost always do whatever the bourgeoisie want. Therefore, workers in first world countries must always stand against their country invading another country. The workers in the first world countries should be in solidarity with the workers in the third world country whose country is being invaded. For example, if the US Army invades a Latin American country the American workers should be against the invasion and their sympathies should be with the Latin American workers, and not with the American war machine. The Latin American workers will rightfully be angry at the American war machine for invading their country. But at the same time that the American war machine is invading their country the Latin American workers must not have any illusions in the bourgeoisie, politicians, and dictators of their own country. The American military may be coming to remove a Latin American politician or dictator, but the Latin American working-class should have no illusions that the Latin American politician or dictator is on their side, because he isn't, and will never be, regardless of whatever rhetoric he says in his speeches. Because the Latin American working class will be rightfully outraged that they have been invaded by a foreign imperialist power the Latin American working class might wish to engage in general strikes and protests and other forms of resistance. But the workers must also be cautious and realistic so that they're not shot down in cold blood. If it's feasible the Latin American workers might wish to do the same to the imperialist invaders that the American people did to the British Redcoats. But during the whole time the Latin American workers should have no illusions in their own "anti-imperialist" bourgeoisie, who when feeling threatened by their own working-class will cooperate with the imperialist American occupation in a second in order to crush the workers. Soldiers in the American army who are against imperialism and against American invasions of other countries should seek to spread anti-imperialist and anti-war consciousness amongst their fellow soldiers. They can point out to their fellow soldiers that the real enemy is back at home, that the real enemy of both workers and rank-and-file soldiers are the war-hungry generals, politicians, and war-profiteers back home. Of course, they may have to be cautious. Who knows, maybe one day one of these invasions or wars will spark the majority of the rank-and-file soldiers of the American military to rebel against the generals, politicians, and multimillionaire war-profiteers who sent them into harms way. Such a rebellion will be more effective if the rank-and-file soldiers are united with the working-class, because united together the workers and soldiers have the power to throw the war-mongering bourgeoisie into the garbage can of history.

Q. Many Third World countries have a large peasant population. How does this affect the workers revolution?

A. The workers and the peasants have the same enemy: the bourgeoisie. The bourgeoisie owns the factories in the cities that pay the workers low wages. The bourgeoisie owns the land in the countryside that pays the peasants poor wages. Both the workers and the peasantry have to unite to get rid of the bourgeoisie through a workers revolution. However, sometimes some peasants can become shortsighted. Understandably they want more land. Specifically, they want the land of the bourgeoisie for themselves. They feel they should have the land because they've worked the land. Indeed, the land must belong to the people, and not to some rich landowner. However, if we just give out the land to the peasants then in the next generation that land will be divided amongst the peasants' children and then the peasants will once again be struggling to survive on smaller and smaller plots of land. The solution to this is the collective or commune. The land that is seized from the rich landowners will be turned into communes or collectives that will pay the peasants wages far superior to anything they were paid by the rich landowners under capitalism. Plus under socialism the peasants will be given quality free medical care like everybody else in the country. In addition, the children of the peasants will receive a quality free education.

Q. What would happen to the small plots of land owned by poor peasants prior to the revolution?

A. They would keep them. Those poor peasants who were lucky enough to have a small piece of land prior to workers revolution would keep their land. However, they could also work on the collectives or communes to make additional money if they would like, at wages far superior than what the large landowners paid the peasants under capitalism.

Q. I'm going to change the subject. You say that is impossible to reform the bourgeois state, that it is impossible to change its bourgeois character through elections. But what about the democracies of the United States and Western Europe – you don't think it's possible to change their bourgeois character through elections?

A. Of course not! At this very moment in Western Europe the bourgeoisie governments there – including those that call themselves pro-worker – are dismantling much of the safety net that gave the Western European workers an enviable standard of living. One of the reasons for that is that the bourgeoisie in these countries no longer feel threatened by the specter of communism anymore now that the Soviet Union has collapsed. They don't feel that they need to buy off the workers anymore with all those social programs. If the Western European workers want to have a good standard of living they're simply going to have to smash the bourgeois state and replace it with a workers state. You can't do this through elections. You can use the elections to make propaganda and point out all the evils of the capitalist system. But if a truly socialist or communist leader wins an election in his country than he should immediately resign. He should not follow in the footsteps of so-called "socialists" or "communists" who once in a bourgeois government betrayed the workers. The only way to achieve a workers state is through workers revolution. The United States is no different. And in Western Europe and the United States just like in other parts of the world the proletariat must not have illusions in the bourgeoisie. The price to pay for illusions in any "progressive" wing of the bourgeoisie is too great! There is no progressive wing of the bourgeoisie! The workers have to smash the bourgeois state and replace it with a workers state through workers revolution. And then the workers state has to smash the bourgeoisie. This is the same everywhere in the world, regardless of whether a bourgeois government takes the form of a bourgeois democracy or a bourgeois dictatorship, regardless if it's the first world or the third world, regardless of whether the country has a history of bourgeois democracy or not. I strongly urge anyone wanting to learn more to read Lenin's *State and Revolution* and Trotsky's *Permanent Revolution.*

The Differences between Trotskyism & Stalinism, Communists & Anarchists, and Why a Socialist & a Communist Are the Same Thing

An Interview with Wolf Larsen

Question: So what is the difference between Trotskyism and Stalinism?

Answer: It all goes back to the Russian Revolution. Lenin and Trotsky were the leaders of the October Revolution in 1917 in Russia. Stalin only played a minor role in the October Revolution. Later, things became very difficult in the Soviet Union. The country was isolated. An attempted workers revolution in Germany in 1919 failed. As time went on the communists like Trotsky who lead the revolution became increasingly isolated within the Soviet Union, and the bureaucracy began to usurp power from the workers and the communists. This bureaucracy wanted to defend its privileged interests, and Joseph Stalin became their leader. Lenin in his *Last Will and Testament* warns about the increasing power of the bureaucracy and their leader Joseph Stalin. Anyway, Joseph Stalin and the bureaucracy imprisoned, exiled, murdered, and sent off to Siberia the very communists who had led the October Revolution in 1917. Leon Trotsky was one of those murdered by the Stalinists. Trotskyists look to the October Revolution in Russia as a shining example of how the working class can liberate itself from the capitalist system. Stalinism, on the other hand, has degenerated into a bizarre multitude of different sects. Some of these sects are outright reformist, like the "Communist" Party USA. The "Communist" Party USA fosters illusions in the Democrats. The endlessly criticize the Republicans, but say little about the Democrats. The Stalinist "Communist" Party USA is basically a left-wing auxiliary of the Democratic Party. How pathetic! Another branch of Stalinism is Maoism. I'll tell you one thing, you never know what those crazy Maoists are going to do!

Q. So explain to us about Maoism.

A. Some of the Maoists foster illusions in the Democrats by pushing an anti-Republican agenda. They don't necessarily say vote for the Democrats but basically they only criticize the Republicans. They hardly criticize the Democrats at all. Other Maoists zig-zag from the left to the right and back again – that is that their politics are all over the place. You never know what crazy irresponsible adventure the Maoists might jump into next. Perhaps this is partly because Chairman Mao was a bit of an adventurer himself, and many of his adventures caused the Chinese people to suffer horribly.

Q. But didn't Mao lead the Chinese people into a successful revolution?

A. It was a successful revolution in the sense that the bourgeoisie was overthrown and Chang Kai-shek and his bloody ruthless Kuomintang were kicked out of mainland China. Kicking the Chinese bourgeoisie out of mainland China helped the Chinese people have a better standard of living. All of that is wonderful! However, because Mao and his organization were Stalinist the Chinese people never enjoyed a workers democracy. Stalinists are not very big on democracy. In Stalinist countries you have a privileged bureaucracy that live like parasites off the workers state. You don't have a workers democracy in Stalinist countries. Besides that, Mao unleashed two horrible idiotic adventures called the Great Leap Forward and the Cultural Revolution. The Great Leap Forward was an attempt to bypass the five-year plans that had been giving China growth rates of 10% a year.

Q. The five-year plans was giving China growth rates of 10% a year?!

A. That's correct. Long before China opened its doors to foreign corporations there was 10% growth rates a year under the five-year plans. China's economy was doing very well. In spite of the fact that the Chinese economy was doing well Mao decided to have this "Great Leap Forward" thing where he threw the five-year plans and the planned economy in the garbage, and he substituted a bunch of crazy irresponsible adventurous nonsense that temporarily ruined the Chinese economy. For this, the Chinese bureaucracy and the other Stalinist hacks in the party basically pushed Mao aside and implemented the five-year plans again and that's when the Chinese economy began to pick up steam again and growth rates reached 10% again. Anyway, Mao didn't like being isolated on the sidelines (at this point he was basically a figurehead without the power he had before) so Mao unleashed the Cultural Revolution in order to get into power again.

Q. So Mao unleashed the Cultural Revolution as a cynical power grab?

A. That's correct. The Cultural Revolution caused all kinds of havoc in China. Plenty of people needlessly suffered. Meanwhile, it was the 1960s and from abroad the Cultural Revolution grabbed the interests of radicals around the world. Certainly the Cultural Revolution was a lot more interesting than anything going on in the Soviet Union at the time. But the Cultural Revolution for those who experienced it was interesting in a very bad way. But from abroad the Cultural Revolution and its slogans and Mao's little red book grabbed a lot of interest.

Q. So that's how a lot of the Maoist groups around the world were born?

A. Yes. So basically a lot of these Maoist groups were born or inspired by all of the craziness of the Cultural Revolution and that crazy adventurer Mao and not surprisingly a lot of Maoist groups can be described as just plain crazy. But at least they're not terrorists – they don't engage in terrorism – thank goodness. It's not impossible that some Maoist group might lead a workers revolution someday, because there are *some* Maoist groups that do not push illusions in the Democrats and other reformist parties. However, I would hope that a Trotskyist party would lead the revolution instead of a Maoist one, because Trotskyists are much more responsible and disciplined. And remember, the October Revolution in Russia in 1917 was very responsible and disciplined. Amongst other things it was relatively free of bloodshed. The bloodshed did not come until later when the Soviet Union was invaded by a number of imperialist armies, and the counterrevolutionary White forces caused a lot of violence and suffering and loss of lives. Capitalist countries like the United States aided the counterrevolutionaries with armaments. Also, a workers state under Trotskyism would be far better. Maoists are basically adventurous Stalinists, and like all the Stalinists they tend to be very uptight about sex. And like I said earlier Stalinists are not big fans of workers democracy. Trotskyists want workers democracy.

Q. But I've noticed that there are a confusing variety of different groups calling themselves Trotskyist. How does one sort it all out?

A. Most so-called Trotskyist groups are reformist – they are Trotskyists in name only. These reformist so-called "Trotskyist" groups basically push illusions in the Democrats or some other reformist party. They seek an alliance with some "progressive" wing of the bourgeoisie. There is no such thing as a quote unquote progressive wing of the bourgeoisie. Leon Trotsky was the co-leader of the Bolshevik Revolution with Lenin. Real Trotskyists want to repeat the October Revolution of 1917 all over the world. That is what Trotskyism is. Trotskyists do not push illusions in reformist leaders or reformist movements or reformist parties. Trotskyists might work with reformist organizations to stop fascist groups like the KKK or the neo-Nazis from marching, Trotskyists might march alongside other reformist groups on a picket line, Trotskyists might defend reformists from government repression. But while doing all these things Trotskyists always maintain their political independence. Trotskyists never push illusions in a reformist leader or reformist movement or reformist party. Real Trotskyists understand that the bourgeoisie state must be smashed, and replaced with a workers state. A Trotskyist understands that there are two classes – the bourgeoisie and the working class – and you're on one side or you're on the other.

Q. A lot of academic socialists would say that all sounds like a bunch of empty slogans. What do you think of academic socialists and their sophisticated analysis of Marxism?

A. It depends on the academic. There are some academics who genuinely believe in workers revolution, but many of these so-called "socialist" academics do not believe in workers revolution. Some of these "socialist" academic types love to play with dialectical materialism and all that endlessly with no practical purpose, and it's a bit like masturbation. It's a bit like contemplating your navel. These academics can contemplate their navels all they want. The Trotskyists will be leading the working class to revolution. Anyone who is a true Marxist is therefore a true Trotskyist. To be a Marxist you have to be a Trotskyist. To be a Leninist you have to be a Trotskyist. Remember, Trotsky was the co-leader of the October Revolution with Lenin. And Trotsky led the resistance to Stalin. Stalin polluted everything Lenin and Marx stood for. Academic drivel that has no practical use is just that – drivel. However, academics who want to be useful can use their knowledge for practical purposes, like helping the working class achieve a revolution. A real socialist academic will write and agitate with the purpose of helping the working class achieve state power through revolution, or at least his writings will help the struggles of workers in some way, perhaps by chronicling the history of workers struggles for example.

Q. What do you say about people who claim to be Marxist, but who say they are not Leninist or Trotskyist?

A. What a bunch of nonsense! It was Lenin and Trotsky who put Marxist ideas into practice in the October Revolution of 1917. Therefore to be a Marxist you must also be a Leninist and a Trotskyist. Generally speaking, people who say they are "Marxist" but renounce Leninism and Trotskyism are people who enjoy playing with Marxism the same way that some academics enjoy playing with it. However, in a practical sense they are against the workers smashing the bourgeoisie through revolution. In other words, they are against the practical application of Marxism, they just want to play around with Marxism.

Q. What do you think of anarchy?

A. Anarchy is complete naïveté, because the anarchists want to do away with the state. If the working class has no state – that is, it has no armed bodies of men with which to defend itself – then the bourgeoisie and their henchmen will slaughter the workers just as they have done infinite times in the past when the workers rebelled. Anarchy sets the workers up to die.

Q. But don't Marxists believes that the state will fade away gradually under communism?

A. In a very far distant future perhaps. But remember right after workers revolution the bourgeoisie are going to be pissed off that all their wealth was taken away from them and used for things like education, public transportation, a cure for AIDS, etc. The former bourgeoisie is not going to be too happy about waking up in the morning and going to work, which is something that a lot of them don't have to do under capitalism. And no doubt some of these bourgeoisie may have stashed away loads of money in secret places. They might be in a position to finance counterrevolution. No doubt many of their former henchmen may still be around and more than happy to help the former bourgeoisie try to reestablish their power through violent means. So in order to stop the former bourgeoisie and their henchmen from making a violent counterrevolution there will have to be a workers state so that the working class has the means to defend itself. In addition, there may be other countries that will still be capitalist for a while, so a workers state will have to have a military in order to defend itself against the possibility of being invaded by capitalist countries intent on restoring the bourgeoisie to power. Therefore, as long as there is the threat of counterrevolution or being invaded the workers must have a state to defend themselves.

Q. What is the difference between a socialist and a communist?

A. There is no difference – they are the same thing. A socialist is a communist and a communist is a socialist. After the workers revolution there will be socialism. Socialism is a transitory stage between capitalism and communism. Communism is a very advanced stage of economic development. I doubt that any of us will live long enough to see communism. However, after a workers revolution we can enjoy socialism. Under socialism everyone will have the right to a job, we will double the minimum wage, there will be free quality medical care and child care, and after capitalism has been wiped off the face of the earth there will be no more war. That's socialism. Since the workers revolution will bring about socialism and in the distant future communism that means socialists and communists are the same thing. Socialists are communists and communists are socialists.

Q. I thought that socialists were more like what has occurred in some Western European countries, and communism is more like what has happened in the Soviet Union and China.

A. Neither socialism or communism has ever been achieved on the planet earth so far. What occurred in the Soviet Union and in China is Stalinism, and Stalinism is neither socialism nor communism. What occurred in Western Europe is not socialism either, what occurred in Western Europe is more like capitalism with a safety net. The workers in Western

Europe fought very hard for their safety net. That's how they got it. The only way to achieve socialism is to have a workers revolution. People who advocate a workers revolution are socialists and communists. A socialist is a communist and a communist is a socialist. The terms are interchangeable.

Watch out for Right-Wing Populist Movements

An Interview with Wolf Larsen

Question: So what are right-wing populist movements?

Answer: Right-wing populist movements are usually led by charismatic figures who receive large donations from the wealthy. These charismatic figures manipulate the frustrations of middle-class people, of working people, and of poor people into mass movements that are or become right-wing and reactionary in nature.

Q. What are the dangers of right-wing Populist movements?

A. Anti-Semitism is one of them. Instead of labeling the bourgeoisie as the perpetrators of endless crimes against the working class and humanity these movements sometimes falsely identify the Jews as being the cause of all the problems in any given society. Some of these right-wing populist movements seek to use Jews or other groups – such as immigrants or gays or minorities – as scapegoats for a society's problems. Of course, in reality it is the bourgeoisie who control any given capitalist country, and it is therefore the bourgeoisie who are responsible for the suffering of the vast majority of people in any given country. But the bourgeoisie seek to put the blame for the problems that capitalism causes on the heads of others. And as I said before these movements are often financed by multimillionaires. The goal of the bourgeoisie is to continue their rule over the workers. They will do so in any manner of different forms, whether it be a bourgeois "welfare state" democracy, or dictatorship, and at times even fascism. A bourgeois government can take many different forms, the main thing the bourgeoisie are concerned about is staying in power and keeping their wealth. One of the means that the bourgeoisie utilize to stay in power is confusing the working people, the unemployed, and the other discontents under capitalism with right-wing populism. Sometimes right-wing populism utilizes religion to confuse the workers. Often times the religious message being spread by these right-wing populists has nothing to do with Jesus Christ or the New Testament or any of that. You only need to read the New Testament in its entirety to realize that many preachers, priests, and right-wing populists pollute the message of Jesus Christ in order to further their own political ends. Not that I'm religious, I'm not. I'm an atheist. But it's absolutely disgusting to see how these right-wing populists often utilize religion in order to blind the working people and mislead them. These right-wing populists cynically use religion to further their own personal ambitions and reactionary political agenda.

Q. So right-wing populism can take a variety of forms. What about left-wing populism?

A. Left-wing populism in some ways is similar to right-wing populism. In other ways it is not. Sometimes it's difficult to tell whether a populist demagogue is right-wing or left-wing or some combination of both. One of the main dangers of left-wing populism is that if the movement or the leader of the movement fosters illusions in the bourgeoisie or in the capitalist system these illusions may in the end cost many of the workers their lives, like what happened in Chile in 1973. Some "left"-wing leaders may be very charismatic and may win over many workers. However, the workers should not allow themselves to be fooled by charisma and great speechmaking. Great speeches and propaganda in the service of proletarian revolution is good, but great speeches that foster illusions in the capitalist system and the bourgeoisie is not. Only a proletarian revolution will bring down the bourgeois state. Only a workers state will have the power to stop the bourgeoisie and their henchmen from drowning the workers in blood. Only a workers party – one similar to the Bolshevik party of Lenin and Trotsky – can lead the workers to revolution. It is foolhardy to follow a left-wing Populist who preaches illusions in the capitalist system or some "progressive" wing of the bourgeoisie.

How I Became a
Communist Sympathizer

An Interview with Wolf Larsen

Question: So when did you get interested in politics?

Answer: The first time I remember being interested in politics was when I was about six years old. I was in Chicago. I was watching a building on the street in front of me burn down. It seemed like buildings were always burning down on the streets in front of our house – much of it was arson – and I could see it all from the window. The buildings in front of our house were part of the ghetto. Anyway, as I watched yet another building burning down I decided I wanted to be the mayor of Chicago, so I could change things.

Q. So you wanted to be mayor of your hometown of Chicago at the age of six – how come you never ran for political office then?

A. Later, when I became older, that is when I became a teenager, I became disgusted with politicians and I changed my mind. I decided I never ever wanted to be a politician!

Q. So you're saying you'll never run for political office?

A. If I ran for political office it would be so that I could talk about the issues facing working-class people and poor people in our country. If I won, I would immediately resign.

Q. Well that would be a first, somebody resigning the minute they won office. Really, that's what you would do?

A. If I ran for political office it would be to talk about racism, or rather the racist oppression of black people, the oppression of gays and women and immigrants, and especially the oppression of working-class people and poor people of all colors. In addition, I would speak out against all these wars. And if I won I would resign – immediately. The reason I would resign is that you can't change the system by just electing another politician. We have to throw the capitalist system in the garbage can – we need a workers revolution.

Q. You sound like a communist. Are you a communist?

A. I've been told that I'm not a communist because I'm not a member of any political group. I don't speak for any political group or tendency. However, I do sympathize with the October Revolution of 1917. I sympathize with the politics of Marx, Engels, Lenin, and Trotsky. I have known communists and have admired them. I do not consider the official so-called quote unquote Communist Party to be communist. They act more like some left-wing auxiliary of the Democrats.

Q. So you're not a communist, but you sympathize with the politics of communism?

A. Yes, that's true.

Q. How long have you been a communist sympathizer?

A. Ever since I was a teenager. Events occurred that made me disgusted with capitalism and capitalist politicians. I worked for the political campaign of Harold Washington when I was quite young – Harold Washington was the first black mayor of Chicago. I think I was 11 years old, who knows, maybe I was the youngest volunteer in his political campaign. Anyway, after he was elected nothing changed – or rather things changed but only for the worse. Chicago begin to hemorrhage good paying union blue-collar jobs, of course it would have happened regardless of whether the mayor was black or white. It was then that I begin to realize that it didn't matter who was in office. The problem is that the capitalist system is inherently awful, and that the capitalist system is a piece of garbage that has to be thrown away. But this is only one factor amongst many that led me to reject the Democratic Party and to move politically leftwards.

Q. What were some of the other factors that led you to reject the Democrats and move leftwards as you put it?

A. Tens of thousands of steel workers losing their jobs at the stroke of some CEO's pen – that was a huge factor in helping me realize that the capitalist system had to go.

Q. Was your family economically affected by the mass layoffs in your hometown?

A. Yes. My family designed machinery for Chicago's industry.

However, compared to the steel workers losing their jobs – well for them it was much worse.

Q. You mentioned that there were many factors that caused you to move leftwards politically as a young person, could you discuss those other factors as well?

A. I grew up in a neighborhood that was completely surrounded by the black ghetto. It was not a white enclave – our neighborhood was racially integrated, and still is. However, being surrounded by poverty from the youngest age definitely helped me see that something was seriously wrong with the status quo. At first, I believed as a child it was possible to reform the system to help the poor and disadvantaged. But when I reached adolescence I realized I was wrong. Before I became an adolescent I had the politics of my parents – liberal Democrat politics – but with adolescence comes independent thinking, and when I started to think for myself I realized that the Democrats were full of shit just like the Republicans.

Q. So being surrounded by poverty as well as mass layoffs in the steel industry in your hometown and dissatisfaction with politicians drove you to the left – anything else?

A. When I was a teenager I began to devour books. At first, I devoured all kinds of books on history and biographies and stuff like that. As time went on I began reading Lenin, Marx, and Engels. I was bored in class so I would often read a book under the desk while the teacher went on about whatever he was going on about. Reading was another factor – a very important factor – that moved me to the left.

Q. And what if anything did you do with your new leftist ideas?

A. At first nothing – I just read and read. I also discussed and argued politics with others, that sort of thing. Then something horrible happened that pushed me into political activism.

Q. What was that horrible thing that helped push you into political activism?

A. In May 1985 Wilson Goode, the first black mayor of Philadelphia, murdered a dozen black activists in cold blood and managed to burn down over 60 homes in a black working-class community in the process. I thought that was really something – the politicians weren't content with bombing innocent people in other countries – now they were bombing Americans. Who bombs their own country? And what irritated me all the more is that most of the white liberals and black nationalists were not even outraged about it – because a black politician did it – a black Democrat. If a white Republican had murdered a dozen black activists on Striver's Row and burned down over 60 homes on Striver's Row in the process you know all those black nationalists and white liberals would be outraged about it – and for good reason. But if a black Democrat murders a dozen black activists it's politically correct – that's disgusting! If a black Democrat is responsible for over 60 homes in a black working-class neighborhood burning to the ground then the white liberals and black nationalists don't say a thing. That's disgusting! I was so disgusted with white liberalism and black nationalism at that point that I became open-minded to left politics. And shortly afterwards I came across a group waving red flags and selling newspapers. They said they were communists. I bought their newspaper and later I became involved with them.

Q. What do you mean you became involved with them?

A. I sold newspapers that were supposedly communist. I talked politics with people – a lot of people. I marched into Marquette Park Chicago which is a white enclave with a couple of other hundred people chanting "Death to the Klan" when the Ku Klux Klan decided to march there. I went to the San Joaquin Valley in California to organize farm workers into a so-called red union. In retrospect, I now realize that group was not communist. I now realize that so-called red unions are bullshit. But I was 16 years old and I didn't know any better.

Q. So your politics have changed?

A. Yes. That first group I was active with was Stalinist. I didn't completely understand the differences between Stalinism and Trotskyism at the time. After all I was only 16 years old. Later I rejected Stalinism. The Stalinists are too uptight about sex! Their politics are similar to the politics of the Stalinist bureaucracy in the Soviet Union – which is enough to make one want to vomit! Trotskyists are more like the original Bolsheviks that led the revolution in Russia in 1917. Trotskyists defend gay rights, they support women's right to an abortion, they're fine with free love, etc. The fact that many of the new-"left"-overs have become such sexual

Puritans made the Trotskyists seem pretty cool to me. The Trotskyists also defended the Soviet Union militarily against the United States, and since we were living in the United States during the period of the Cold War I thought that was pretty brave! It made sense to me. The Stalinist bureaucracy had to go – but not the Soviet Union – not the worker's state itself.

Q. But isn't that irrelevant now that the Soviet Union has collapsed?

A. No. Because the same groups that were too weak to defend the Soviet Union during the Cold War will be too weak to take principled stands on issues both in the present and in the future. I remember when I was a student at the University of Wisconsin-Madison that at rallies people would be chanting "Let the communist speak! Let the communist speak!" because the liberals never wanted to let us speak out in opposition to the Cold War.

Q. Really? The liberals supported the Cold War?

A. Yes they did. The liberals were firmly committed to the Democrats and the Democrats were firmly committed to the Cold War. The Democrats and liberals were just as anti-Communist or almost as anti-Communist as the right-wing conservative Republicans that they were constantly criticizing. Liberals hate to have their politics attacked from the left! Liberals often trample upon the free speech rights of those who criticize them from the left – at least that was my experience when I was politically active.

Q. So you're not politically active anymore?

A. No, but maybe that will change.

Q. I understand that you're a writer. Could you talk about some of the other books you've written.

A. All of the books I've written so far have been very different than this one. Only some of those books are conventional – meaning that they have a traditional plot. Two of my books are mostly autobiographical – those books are *Unalaska Alaska* and *Travel around the World? Why Not?* Then I have a lot of other books which are neither conventional nor autobiographical – they are experimental works of prose, poetry, theater, and whatnot. These are often works of imagination. They are not realistic. They're meant to take the reader into a kind of fantasy world. They're meant to help the reader temporarily escape the drudgery and realities of life. As much as possible I try to make these works fun for the reader. However, I do not live in a vacuum. The horrible nightmare of the world we live in today to some extent affects what I write. So some of my creative works have a nightmarish quality to them because the world we live in is a nightmare.

Q. Why do you say the world is a nightmare?

A. I've traveled to over 50 countries. I've seen a lot of suffering. On top of that there is simply too much war. And it's scary to think that the United States and Russia still have huge stockpiles of nuclear weapons that threaten the human race with extinction. It's a nightmare. There are so many beautiful things in the world, but there are a lot of problems in the world as well. There are so many things that must be changed. Change will come from the working-class. The working class has the power to change the world.

Race in America is Impossible

An Essay by Wolf Larsen

Race in America is impossible. Black workers, white workers, and latin workers are divided against each other. This division is fostered by white racists, black nationalists, and the news media. The white, black, and latin workers are thus divided and conquered. White and black workers vote for the Democratic Party – but the Democratic Party is the enemy of working people just like the Republicans. Black faces in high places has changed nothing for working-class blacks. While some blacks have risen to some of the most powerful positions in our country the fact is many blacks have been left behind to suffer in poverty. Blacks who have positions of power have often used that power to oppress working class and poor blacks.

Some black people are wealthier than ever. Some black people have more power than ever. But many black workers and poor blacks are worse off than before. Similarly, many white workers and many poor whites are also worse off than before.

A liberal white elite and most of the black elite continue to push the illusion that the Democrats are the friend of black people. This is only partly true. The Democrats are the friends of a small black elite with money and power. The Democrats, just like the Republicans, are the enemies of working class and poor blacks.

Let us not forget that it was the Democrats that opposed the Emancipation Proclamation during the Civil War. It was the Democrats that opposed the North making civil war against the South. It was the Democrats, with the help of some moderate Republicans, who ended Reconstruction.

It all goes back to the Civil War. If the Democrats had not ended Reconstruction black people may have achieved equality with whites in the 19th century! During Reconstruction black people achieved wonderful gains! However, because the Democrats ended Reconstruction black people have suffered another hundred years of brutal racist oppression.

How is somebody going to say that the Democrats are more for black people when the Democrats wanted to maintain blacks as slaves? If the Democrats had had their way black people wouldn't be living in the United States of America – they would be living in the Confederate States of America. The Democrats wanted to let the Confederacy secede from the United States! And many of the Confederate flag emblems on the state flags throughout the South were put there by the Democratic Party.

The fact is the Democratic Party is a party of Uncle Tom politicians, the KKK, Jim Crow segregation, and lynching.

That is the history of the Democratic Party. The Democratic Party is not the friend of black people.

The fact that the Democrats put black faces in very high places changes nothing. Throughout American history white cops and white judges and white politicians waged a war against black people. Black men were brutalized, poor black men were thrown in jail for crimes they did not commit, and many black men were shot down in the streets by trigger-happy white cops. Now, there are black cops shooting down innocent black men in the streets. There are also black judges sentencing innocent black man to jail – where they are often raped! And what the black politicians are doing to black people today is no different than what white politicians have been doing to black people for hundreds of years.

Black politicians keep down black people just like white politicians. The most infamous example of this is the MOVE bombing in Philadelphia in May 1985. The black mayor of Philadelphia ordered a bomb to be dropped on a black organization called MOVE. The bombing murdered a dozen black activists and their children. Over 60 black working-class homes in the black neighborhood burned down to the ground as a result of the bombing.

I remember May 1985. I remember what made black nationalist men angry in May 1985. I'm a white man and back in May 1985 my girlfriend was black. Back in May 1985 wherever I went with my black girlfriend the black nationalists whined: "Oh sister and white man – what are you guys doing together?! WAAAAAAAAAA!" However, in May 1985 I didn't hear a single black nationalist complain about a black mayor murdering a dozen black activists in cold blood and burning down over 60 black working-class homes in the process.

I guess they don't make black nationalists like they used to. Malcolm X said: "When you vote Democrat you vote Dixiecrat!" Malcolm X was murdered in cold blood by other black nationalists. Black nationalists are inherently racist, but with some exceptions (like Malcolm X and the Black Panthers) most black nationalists are NOT militant at all.

It is ironic that black nationalists call other people "sellouts" and "Uncle Toms", when most black nationalists are hustling the black vote for a Democratic Party that opposed the Emancipation Proclamation, ended Reconstruction, and enforced Jim Crow on generations of blacks. For years the Democratic Party was the favorite political party of the Ku Klux Klan! So if the black nationalists want to know who the "sellouts" and "Uncle Toms" are than they just need to look in the mirror.

The Democratic Party may even select a black man or woman as its presidential candidate. What difference does it make to an innocent black man being raped in prison tonight if the President of the United States is black? What difference does it make to a homeless black man living under a bridge that the President is black? What difference does it make to a black man that's unemployed, to another black man making minimum wage without benefits, and another black man who can't afford medical care copayments that the President is black?

I am a white man. I have been homeless. I worked manual labor for 12 years. I have waited for hours and hours at public hospitals in vain trying to get medical care. I have worked for minimum wage. It didn't make a damn bit of difference to me that the President was white.

Working class and poor black people urgently need real change in this country, just like working class and poor whites urgently need real change too.

Working class whites and blacks have many of the same struggles. Poor whites and blacks have many of the same struggles too! Medical care is increasingly becoming a privilege for the rich. We are at the mercy of insurance companies! Wages are stagnant. We work hard and we get little in return. The cost of living keeps going up, rents keep going up, gasoline keeps going up, food costs keep going up, and yet it doesn't seem that wages are keeping up.

If a white worker doesn't have enough money to put gasoline in his tank so he can drive to work, and he can't afford medical care for himself and his family, and his rent goes up and up and he can't afford it should he take pride that the President of the United States is white? Obviously the answer is no! And if the President of the United States is black and if you're a black man struggling to pay rent, medical care, and all those other bills and those stagnant wages just aren't keeping up with the rising cost of living should you give a damn whether the President is white or black?

Where do working class and poor blacks go from here?

Should they identify with the aspirations of the black elite? Other than skin color what do working class and poor blacks have in common with the black elite? Other than skin color what do working class and poor whites have in common with the white elite?

The fact is black people struggling to pay the bills and working for low wages have nothing in common with a black elite that drives luxury automobiles and has an entirely different lifestyle. If you have to pull out a credit card and go further in debt just to pay your grocery bill than what do you have in common with someone eating caviar?

There are some black people – a very small number of black people – who argue that blacks should vote Republican. Their argument seems to be that since the Republicans actually did something for black people over 150 years ago that that's good enough reason for the black people to vote Republican.

If this was the 1860s then yes it would be a good idea to vote Republican. Because back in the 1860s the Republican Party was doing positive things for black people – like Reconstruction, like the Emancipation Proclamation, and like smashing the Confederacy with the Union Army.

But a long time has passed since the 1860s. And the Republican Party hasn't done a damn thing for black people since. And that's why black people should not bother with the Republican Party.

So what should black people do – or rather what should

black workers and black poor people do? If neither the Democrats or the Republicans are doing a damn thing for black people than what should black people do?

Black people need a third party. Most white people need a third party too. But what kind of third party? We certainly don't need the Green party! The Green Party puts the rights of animals before the rights of workers! How ridiculous! There's all kinds of third parties out there that do not represent the interests of workers.

What both black and white workers need is a workers party. A party that will fight for workers of all colors. A workers party must pay special attention to the double oppression suffered by black workers in this country. A workers party must fight for racial equality for black people. White workers need to understand that black people have experienced four centuries of brutal racist oppression.

I worked as a longshoreman for 10 years. A longshoreman is a dockworker. My union racially integrated the docks back in the 1930s, thus giving black dockworkers more equality. The fact that black and white workers thus worked together and were united in fighting a common struggle against the shipping bosses made it possible for me to make good wages. I also had a certain degree of job security. I couldn't be fired just because some lame foremen didn't like me. It also helps that a black coworker saved me one day when an accident on the job nearly occurred. If it hadn't been for that black coworker I would have been paralyzed from the waist down.

Besides watching each other's backs on the job black and white workers benefit from higher wages and better benefits when they fight together instead of against each other. A workers party would extend the struggle of workers into the political sphere. Thus, black and white workers together could fight for things like free quality medical care for all.

Let us not forget that the United States of America was founded by slaveholders and slave traders. Black people will never achieve liberation and equality as long as they are ruled by a government founded by slaveholders and slave traders. What black workers need is nothing less than a workers party. White and latino workers need the same thing – a workers party.

The Woman's Question

An Essay by Wolf Larsen

Women in the United States of America and all over the world are treated like second-class citizens. There is no shortage of political correctness and feminism, but this is just a bunch of worthless window-dressing that fails to address critical issues facing working-class women.

Feminists whine about pornography and that men are not much better than dogs. Personally, I worked in a predominately male environment for 12 years. And I can't understand why anybody would insult dogs by comparing them to men. But seriously, what's wrong with nudity? What's wrong with movies showing people having sex? Frankly, I can't think of anything more natural than nudity and sex. The fact is is that many feminists – at least in the United States of America – are a bunch of Puritans! They are Puritans just like those crazy religious-fanatics that came over on the Pilgrim ship and founded our neurotic country – which remains Puritanical to this day.

The fact that many of these feminists have adopted the puritanical values of religious extremists is nothing less than treason when one considers that religious extremists are hostile to women's rights. How strange that these feminists that supposedly support the struggle for women's rights have the same puritanical anti-sexual values as the born-again Christians who stand outside abortion clinics and harass women who are exercising their right to abortion.

Even the feminist slogan of "freedom of choice" is weak. It is imperative to launch an all-out struggle to defend the right of women to have free abortion on demand! Poor women should have the right to an abortion too!

A struggle to defend women's right to an abortion would involve asking labor unions, workers, progressive students, women, etc. to come out and defend abortion clinics by any means necessary against these religious bigots who are trying to deny women their right to an abortion. It is not enough that women have the right to an abortion on paper. We must defend abortion clinics against these religious-extremist bigots.

Just as it is imperative to defend abortion clinics it is important to fight to make contraception available for free to all females of reproductive age. In this day and age with HIV running rampant it is important that condoms be available to all for free! Condoms must be distributed in both high schools and middle schools! Free condom dispensing machines should be available on every street corner in every nation across the world.

Sexuality must be treated as something natural. We must throw away all those feminist and born-again Christian puritanical values. Once we treat sexuality as something natural we began to understand the need for distributing free condoms to everyone, the need to fight for free abortion on demand, and the need to spend more money on a cure for AIDS and less money on war. In fact, no money should go to war.

One of the major obstacles to achieving women's liberation is illusions in the Democratic Party. There have been lots of Democratic presidents. The Democratic Party has done next to nothing for women. We still don't have equal pay for equal work. We still don't have quality free child care for working women. We still don't have free abortion on demand. In fact, there are more and more places in America where it is difficult for women to get an abortion because of a lack of facilities. And if you think having a woman as President is going to change that or anything else look no further than the example of England's Margaret Thatcher to understand that female politicians are no different than male politicians.

What is needed is a workers party! A workers party will fight for the rights of working women. A workers party will fight for free abortion on demand, free contraceptives available to all, free quality child care for all working women, and equal pay for equal work.

Ultimately, the goal is complete equality for women. Ultimately, the goal is women's liberation!

To achieve women's liberation we must completely change this nation that was founded by anti-sexual Puritans. To achieve women's liberation we must live in a society where women have control of their own bodies. For women to have control of their own bodies and their own destinies women must have full control over their own reproductive rights. For women to have control of their own reproductive rights we must smash the puritanical forces who seek to deny women the right to an abortion. We must struggle against puritanical forces who seek to deny women the right to free contraceptives. All females of reproductive age must have access to free contraceptives regardless of age. If you are old enough to get pregnant you should have the right to acquire free contraceptives.

The forces of Puritanism are the enemy of women. Teenage girls get pregnant because they are not taught about birth control. They are only taught abstinence. Telling teenagers not to have sex is like telling a shark not to eat fish. Teenagers must have the right to learn about sexuality in school, and they should have the right to free contraceptives so they won't get pregnant.

The puritanical forces that are worried that teenagers might have sex are the same right-wing forces that usually support war. Their Christian morality says teenage sex is bad but war is okay. This kind of "morality" is diabolical.

Let us not forget that it was the Puritans that founded this nation. In order to end the Puritan rule that keeps women down we need fundamental change – we need something besides the same old Democrats and Republicans – we need a workers party that will fight for women's liberation and women's equality and women's rights!

I Support Gay Rights 100% and So Should You!!

An Essay by Wolf Larsen

I think the major difference between straight people and gay people is that straight people make lots of babies and gay people don't. Is there a shortage of babies on this planet? Some people argue that homosexuality isn't "natural" – is that because a homosexual couple can't make babies? But isn't there already enough babies as it is?

Bigots are against gay marriage. But if you look up gay in the dictionary you will find gay means happy. And there's lots of unhappy marriages! So what's the problem? Gays should have every right to be married and miserable like straight people!

All jokes aside gays should be treated with respect. Gays should have all the same rights as straight people. Since gay men tend to dress nicer, groom themselves better, and get along with women better than straight men I can't imagine why any heterosexual man would want these good-looking men to be straight. In fact, I figure the more gay guys the merrier for me – because that means all the more women for me!

But seriously, there's nothing more cowardly than a group of straight men attacking one gay man or two gay men. Gay men have an undeserved reputation for being meek – but if that's so how come it takes a dozen straight bigots to beat up two gay men? It must be that the bigots are the ones who are weak and cowardly – and ignorant too! I'm a strong believer in the Second Amendment. It's important that gays have the right to defend themselves against violent homophobic bigots.

Straight workers must fight for full equality rights for gay workers. Straight workers must fight against homophobic discrimination on the job. Think about it – if management can get away with discriminating against gays then that means they can get away with discriminating against blacks, Latinos, women, and anybody else they don't like. It is in the self-interest of straight workers to defend gay workers. All workers must remember that an injury to one is an injury to all! Even if you're a straight white man you should defend homosexuals. If management can get away with firing or discriminating against somebody because they're gay – then maybe tomorrow management will fire you or discriminate against you just because they don't like your personality! I am a straight white male – and in spite of showing up on time every day and always working without an excuse in all kinds of weather and always doing my job – I still found myself afoul of management now and then – probably because I speak my mind. I had a union job, and I am glad that management couldn't fire people just because they were gay or they were black or because they spoke out about certain problems on the job.

The fact is gays are used as scapegoats. If you're frustrated because your job is paying you peanuts, because your rent is too high, because you're always stuck in traffic, because blah blah blah – you shouldn't take out your frustrations on someone just because they're gay – just because they prefer somebody of the same gender. Who cares if someone prefers another person of the same gender – what does it matter to you? What does somebody else's sexual preferences have to do with paying your bills or any of your other problems?

If you're a worker than you should support the struggle of gay workers for full equality. Why? Because they're workers just like you! Besides, if you support their struggle, then they'll support your struggle. If you're black you should support the struggle of women and gays and Latinos for equality – so that they'll support your struggle for equality too! If you're a woman then you should support the struggle for gay rights for the same reason. If you're a straight white male worker then you should support the struggle of gay workers for full equality for the simple reason that they are workers – just like you.

The Democratic Party Is Just As Rotten As the Republican Party!

An Essay by Wolf Larsen

The Democratic Party is the enemy of working people. The Democratic Party represents the liberal wing of the rich. Hence, the Democrats are just as anti-union and anti-worker as the Republican Party. Democratic politicians support strikebreaking legislation just like the Republicans. Democratic politicians talk peace but they make war. Democrats pretend to be the friends of working people – but the Democrats are liars.

The Democrats escalated the war in Vietnam, initiated the blockade to starve Cuba, and brought the world to the brink of a nuclear war during the Cuban missile crisis. It was the Democrats that dropped the atomic bomb on Hiroshima and Nagasaki. The Democrats are a party of war, just like the Republicans.

Many liberals and conservatives alike will tell you that it was "necessary" to drop the atomic bomb on Hiroshima and Nagasaki. Nonsense! Japan was already finished as a military power prior to the nuclear holocaust of Hiroshima and Nagasaki. Many liberals and conservatives alike argue that it would have cost many American lives to invade the Japanese islands prior to the bombing of Hiroshima and Nagasaki. Invade the Japanese islands? What for? If the purpose of the war was to stop Japanese aggression rather than make aggression against Japan then why invade the Japanese islands? Japan had already been reduced to rubble by American bombing campaigns, and Japan had already been kicked out of one country after another by the Allied troops. Perhaps America had its own aggressive agenda on Japan. Or perhaps the Democrat Harry Truman dropped the atomic bomb on Hiroshima and Nagasaki as an experiment – a war experiment – an experiment to see how many people their new war toy would kill! In addition, the Democrat President Harry Truman wanted to send a message to the world: we're the new superpower, obey us or else!

So the fact is the Democrats, who dropped the atomic bomb on Hiroshima and Nagasaki, are war criminals just like the Republicans. It was the Democrats who escalated the war in Vietnam. Many many Vietnamese died during the Vietnam War. What the American war machine and the Democrats did to the people of Vietnam is nothing less than a huge war crime! Dropping bombs from the air, dropping napalm on the people, burning down villages, killing innocent civilians, and making Vietnam's South little more than an American colony are just some of the crimes that the Democrats presided over in Vietnam.

Consider the history of the Democratic Party. Prior to, during, and after the Civil War the Democrats campaigned as "the white man's party". The Democrats were an unabashedly racist party from the very beginning! The Democrats opposed the North making civil war against the South. The Democrats wanted to let the South succeed from the Union. If the Democrats had had their way black people would not be living in the United States of America – if the Democrats had had their way black people would be living in the Confederate States of America!

In addition, or rather to add insult to injury, the Democrats opposed the Emancipation Proclamation. If the Democrats had their way black people would never have been set free from chattel slavery! The Democrats opposed Reconstruction. It was during Reconstruction that black people made the greatest progress that they had ever made in American history. It was the Democrats – along with the help of some moderate Republicans – who ended Reconstruction. Thus the Democrats are directly responsible for the fact that black people continue to experience brutal racist oppression to this day! How black nationalists can argue that the Democrats are more for black people is beyond me! Other black nationalists like Malcolm X argued, "When you vote Democrat you vote Dixiecrat!" Unlike most black nationalists Malcolm X was actually militant. I disagree with many things that Malcolm X said but when he talked about politicians he was often right on the money! And when Malcolm X talked about black politicians he referred to them as Uncle Toms, collaborators in a racist system, and lots of other worse things. Malcolm X hated politicians both black and white of both parties. If Malcolm X were alive today and if he still had the same politics he would denounce Barack Obama as a collaborator of the racist system that keeps black people down.

The Democrats pretend to be the friends of workers – both black and white. The Democrats have done nothing for workers. In fact the Democrats support strikebreaking legislation just like the Republicans. If you go on strike and your strike is having great success don't be surprised if a Democratic politician calls out the National Guard to smash your picket line and escort the scabs in.

There is one difference between the Republicans and the Democrats. The Democrats love to patronize working-class people in America. The Democrats like to come down to your job, put on a hardhat, and say some pretty words to the press about working people. But they just say all that to get elected! And after they get elected they pretty much do the same as the Republicans.

Democrats say pretty words about women's rights, but they never actually deliver women's rights. All the Democrats care about is getting women's votes. I remember when I was young – very young. I was in junior high and just entering puberty. The Democrats and the feminists were talking all this blah blah blah about equal pay for equal work. I'm now a balding middle-aged man and guess what – we still don't have equal pay for equal work! So many Democrat administrations have come and gone, so many Democrat controlled congresses have come and gone, and still no equal pay for equal work.

The struggle for women's liberation and women's rights begins with rejecting both the Democratic and Republican parties. We need a third party! We need a workers party that will fight for the rights of working women! We need a workers party that will fight for equal pay for equal work, we need a workers party that will fight for free abortion on demand, we need a workers party that will fight for free quality child care for all working women, we need a workers party that will fight to restore welfare for poor women and their children, we need a workers party that will fight for free contraception for all females of reproductive age. In order to have women's equality and liberation we need a workers party! A workers party will also fight for gay rights, as well as equality for blacks and immigrants as well. A workers party will fight for all workers of all skin colors.

Capitalism and World War III

An Interview with Wolf Larsen

Question: So, do you think that World War III is possible?

Answer: Yes, I do. In fact, not only do I think it's possible I think it's probable.

Q. Why do you think that a nuclear war is probable?

A. Look, the Cold War may be over, but the stockpiles of nuclear weapons are still sitting there. They're sitting there for a reason.

Q. What reason is that?

A. The stockpiles of nuclear weapons are sitting there waiting for World War III. It's impossible to say – or difficult to say – which countries will be on which side. But war is always. Under the capitalist system there is always war.

Q. Well, it's true that there has been a lot of war. The last century alone saw two world wars. But don't you think that because World War III will be so horrible – because of nuclear weapons and all – that therefore World War III will never happen? Because it will be too horrible?

A. The problem with that argument is that people made the same argument prior to World War I. In the years immediately preceding World War I there were those who were warning that a world war – or a war between the major European powers – was nearly imminent. Other people dismissed those warnings as being overly alarmist. These people argued that all the new advancements in warfare had made war unthinkable – and that therefore there would be no war. But these people were wrong. World War I happened anyway, and it turned out to be more horrible than anybody imagined.

Q. But the United States and Russia have just signed a treaty to reduce their weapons. Don't you think that with all the peace agreements and the end of the Cold War and the collapse of the Soviet Union that we will now be entering an era of peace?

A. That's just it! We haven't entered a period of peace! The Cold War is over yet still there is endless war! The United States right now is in two wars at the same time – in Afghanistan and in Iraq. As far as peace treaties go the period preceding World War I saw endless peace treaties and endless disarmament treaties and yet that didn't stop World War I from happening.

Q. You keep mentioning World War I. Why do you keep mentioning World War I?

A. I keep mentioning World War I because World War I was a horrible carnage! Many people considered it senseless. However, war is endless under capitalism. It's the nature of the capitalist system to bring endless war. In addition, the situation in the world today resembles the situation before World War I in many ways.

Q. You say the situation today resembles in many ways the situation before World War I. How is that?

A. Prior to World War I there was intense competition between the various powers of Europe for markets and economic domination and whatnot. Today it is not much different. There is intense competition between the major world powers for global markets. Trade wars lead to shooting wars. The origins of many wars are economic. The competition between two or more superpowers heats up and so they go to war. The collapse of the Soviet Union only made the economic competition between the various capitalistic powers even more intense. The major capitalist powers were united against the Soviet Union. But now all the major capitalistic powers do not have a common enemy. And the competition between the United States and its former allies on the other side of the Atlantic is heating up. Economic competition leads to economic wars which lead to shooting wars.

Q. Economic competition between different superpowers throughout history has led to war, that is true. But still, don't you think the use of atomic weapons would just be too horrible for anyone to consider using them first?

A. The war-mongering nuts in the White House have already used the atomic bomb – in Hiroshima and Nagasaki. If they're crazy enough to use the atomic bomb once they're crazy enough to use it again. If the United States government is crazy enough to create a huge stockpile of nuclear weapons they're crazy enough to use it. The US government has never renounced the first use of nuclear weapons. The Soviet Union – back when it existed – did renounce the first use of nuclear weapons. The Soviet Union stockpiled nuclear weapons to defend itself from the United States. If the Soviet Union had not had that huge stockpile of nuclear weapons then the United States might have dropped the atomic bomb on cities like Moscow and also Hanoi in Vietnam.

Q. You really think that the US government would have dropped the atomic bomb on Hanoi in Vietnam?

A. Yes, I do believe so. Because the United States was losing the war. The only way that they could've brought the North Vietnamese government to their knees is dropping the atomic bomb on Hanoi. But, dropping the atomic bomb on Hanoi might have begun World War III with the Soviet Union.

Q. But doesn't the very fact that the United States government did not drop the atomic bomb on Hanoi prove that the US government is not crazy enough to use the atomic bomb again?

A. The US government decided it wasn't worth it to have a nuclear war with the Soviet Union over Vietnam. However, when the situation came much closer to home the United States was willing to have a nuclear war. John F. Kennedy brought the world to the brink of a nuclear holocaust during the Cuban missile crisis. It was Khrushchev that backed down, not Kennedy. If Khrushchev had not backed down during the Cuban missile crisis there might have been a nuclear war. And if there had been a nuclear war we would not exist today.

Q. I see, but even if there is a nuclear war do you think it will be as horrible as many say it will be? Isn't it possible that the human race will survive a nuclear war?

A. If there is a limited exchange – such as if India and Pakistan had a nuclear war – there would be widespread nuclear contamination and many people all over the world might get radiation sickness and cancer and die. But it's still doubtful that the entire human race would go extinct if the nuclear war is between countries with smaller arsenals of nuclear weapons like India and Pakistan. However, in the event of a nuclear war between two countries with heavy stockpiles of nuclear weapons like Russia and the United States then I do believe it's probable that the human race will go extinct. The people in the United States and Russia would die quickly – in many cases instantaneously. The rest of the human race – the people outside Russia and the United States – would die slowly, but they would all probably die. There would simply be too much nuclear radiation contaminating everything – including the air the water the ground and all the plants and fish and animals we eat as well. Everything would be contaminated with nuclear radiation. In addition, a major nuclear war would cause so much destruction and therefore cause so much dust in the atmosphere that it would block out the rays of the sun. This in turn would kill off the plant life and the large-scale die off of plant life across the world would cause a large-scale die off of animals – so all the animals and plants that we eat would be dead. So even if someone were lucky enough to be immune to all of the nuclear radiation in the sea and the air and the water they still wouldn't have anything to eat. So they would die. So a nuclear war would not only cause massive numbers of people to die of radiation poisoning, but it would also cause massive deaths from starvation. If you still doubt that a major nuclear war would cause human extinction then you should go to the Peace Museum in Hiroshima. See with your own eyes what one primitive nuclear bomb can do. Remember, today's nuclear weapons are far more powerful than the ones used in Hiroshima and Nagasaki. And only one nuclear bomb was dropped on Hiroshima, and it destroyed a good part of the city.

Q. Have you been to the Peace Museum in Hiroshima?

A. Yes, I have. From the photographs it became obvious that the one primitive nuclear bomb used destroyed a good part of the city. In addition, the survivors had been asked to paint and draw what they saw immediately after the dropping of the atomic bomb. The pictures you see are a horrible scene. The drawings are of people with their arms spread away from their bodies because the flesh from their arms and their bodies was flowing down to the ground and if they had their arms next to their bodies then their arms would stick to their bodies. So all these people with their flesh oozing off of their bodies were walking in mass to the river as they groaned "Water! Water! Water!" over and over again and when they reached the river they drank and drank the water and then they died. There were massive numbers of corpses flowing down the river of Hiroshima. The nuclear bombs of today are so numerous and much much more powerful.

Q. But what about the possibility of a terrorist dirty bomb? Doesn't that seem far more likely than a major nuclear war?

A. I don't have a crystal ball. So it's impossible for me to say whether there will be a terrorist "dirty-bomb" or not. That would certainly be horrible. However, it will not cause the human race to go extinct. While the idea of a "dirty-bomb" is terrifying the idea of the extinction of the human race from a major nuclear war is also terrifying – far more terrifying. What's interesting is that our government – the United States government – uses the fear of a "dirty-bomb" and terrorism in general to justify limiting many of our civil liberties. What's ironic about all of this is that here's the United States government talking about the dangers of a possible nuclear bomb when in fact the United States government has the biggest stockpile of nuclear weapons in the entire world! The United States government is the biggest terrorist in the world. The huge stockpile of nuclear weapons of the United States government is the biggest threat to the survival of mankind, as well as the huge stockpile in Russia's hands as well. Homo sapiens have been the only humans on this planet for the past 30,000 years, because 30,000 years ago Neanderthal went extinct. Do you think we can survive another 30,000 years with the atomic bomb? So far, we've managed to survive some 65 years with the atomic bomb. Do you think we could survive another 650 years with the atomic bomb? Do you think we could survive another 6,500 years with the atomic bomb? Do we want our descendents to be destroyed in a nuclear war?

Q. So what do you think should be done to eliminate new weapons? Or rather, is it feasible to eliminate nuclear weapons?

A. We *have* to eliminate nuclear weapons, or otherwise eventually at some point in the future there will be a major nuclear war and the human race will go extinct. And even if the human race doesn't go extinct from a nuclear war civilization as we know it will cease to exist, and there will be huge die offs of human beings. The entire world would be contaminated with nuclear cancer-causing fallout. The number of births defects would be staggering. It would just be so horrible that we must do everything possible to eliminate nuclear weapons from the world. So you see, it is not a question of whether it's feasible or not to eliminate nuclear weapons – we must do it!

Q. But you didn't answer my first question. How do we eliminate nuclear weapons? Don't you think our own government – the US government – is doing its best to eliminate nuclear weapons? After all, our government is doing everything possible it can to stop the proliferation of nuclear weapons. Our government is doing everything it can to stop Iran and North Korea from acquiring nuclear weapons. And on top of that our government has signed a treaty with Russia to eliminate some of the nuclear weapons in both nations' stockpiles.

A. The key word there is some. The treaty only eliminates about a third of the nuclear stockpiles of Russia and the United States. So there will still be plenty of nuclear weapons there to kill off the entire human race – or to at least kill off most of the human race. Remember, the nuclear nuts in the White House have a bomb shelter to escape to. So maybe they think they can survive a nuclear war, I don't know, but the people running the world are a bunch of crazy war-mongering fools, and they certainly can't be trusted with the atomic button. As far as the anti-proliferation efforts of the United States government against North Korea and Iran is concerned it is rather hypocritical for the country with the highest stockpile of nuclear weapons in the world to be telling other countries that they can't have nuclear weapons. Especially when our own government acts like a big bully threatening countries like North Korea and Iran those countries feel that they need to arm themselves with a nuclear bomb to protect themselves from an American invasion.

Q. Then what should be done to eliminate nuclear weapons – all nuclear weapons – from the world?

A. The solution is to get rid of capitalism. Capitalism brings endless war. We should take both the war-mongering Democrats and Republicans and throw them out of government and let them pick up garbage off the streets for food stamps. (Laughs) Or they can do something else for a living. But I tell you in order to bring about world peace the Democrats and Republicans will both have to get new jobs. We should throw them out of the government. Remember that it was the Democrats who dropped the atomic bomb on Hiroshima and Nagasaki – that was Harry Truman. Remember that it was the Democrats that brought the world to the brink of a nuclear holocaust during the Cuban missile crisis – that was John F. Kennedy. So either the Democrats and the Republicans might push the atomic button. The only solution is to kick the Democrats and Republicans out of office. What we need is a workers party. A workers party will bring peace. Once there are workers parties in power in countries throughout the world we will be able to eliminate nuclear weapons from the face of the earth.

Q. Only once the world is ruled by workers parties – and only then – will it be possible to eliminate nuclear weapons from the face of the earth? Really?

A. Yes, I believe so. Capitalism brings endless war. A socialist nation might need nuclear weapons in order to defend itself from capitalist nations, that is to keep the capitalist nations at bay. But once there are no more capitalist countries on the planet then it will be possible to eliminate nuclear weapons for good. Once capitalism no longer exists on the planet earth there will be no more war.

www.ingramcontent.com/pod-product-compliance
Lightning Source LLC
Chambersburg PA
CBHW030312290526
45785CB00001B/315